REVIVAL

Volume Two

REVIVAL SANCTUARY®
FOR WOMEN IN BUSINESS

Sharon Brown

Published by

P E A C H E S

P U B L I C A T I O N S

Published in London by Peaches Publications, 2021.
www.peachespublications.co.uk

The moral right of the author has been asserted.

British Library Cataloguing in Publication Data: A catalogue record for this book is available from the British Library.

ISBN: 9781838401801

Book cover design: Deearo Marketing.
Editor: Linda Green.
Typesetter: Winsome Duncan.
Proofreader: Linda Green.

TABLE OF CONTENTS

Table of Contents

DEDICATION

This book is dedicated to my mum, Lydia who continues to inspire, motivate and believe in me through every hurdle and challenge.

ACKNOWLEDGEMENTS

To the women business owners within this book who saw an opportunity to share their stories and become a published Author and to make a difference to help others through their own experiences.

To my community, Revival Sanctuary and all of those loyal and dedicated members within it who continue to encourage each other and me every day to be the best versions of themselves.

To Peaches Publications, my publisher, thank you for your efficiency, guidance and opportunity to publish this second edition in the way we are doing it.

To Marcia M Spence, the publisher for Revival (volume one), for educating me on how I could take the digital version of these books to published versions and being our very first publisher.

To my family and friends who support me every day in my quest to succeed and get out of my comfort zone.

THANK YOU

FOREWORD

By Aly Jones

Sharon is an inspiring, action taking power-house of fantastic ideas with an excellent ethos, ensuring she always delivers on her promise.

She has been successful in creating and offering a wonderfully cooperative and heart centred community, providing a way to embrace a new way of networking that allows space for all members to respect, trust and support one another in a collaborative rather than a competitive way.

Through her own unfulfilling experiences at work and with networking, Sharon felt strongly about providing a new and special way of supporting her community.

Sharon is a continuous hive of creative ideas and goes the extra mile every time to ensure she leads her tribe with integrity, compassion, fairness and honesty. Sharon actively encourages business engagement between her members both here and internationally, but also offers many opportunities for not only her members, but also non-members to get involved in other open projects including: Co-authoring, Retreats, Article Writing, Event Hosting, Speaking and Project Directing to name but a few!

Sharon doesn't stop and is always thinking of new ways and new ideas to offer the community, and is currently leading opportunities in several collaborative book, magazine, events, hosting and public speaking projects, and is also working on her latest idea of a CIC for a corporate anti bullying initiative.

INTRODUCTION

By Sharon Brown

www.revivalsanctuary.co.uk
sharon@revivalsanctuary.co.uk

CREATING A MOVEMENT

t's strange how ideas hit you. One simple thought can go in so many directions and without action it remains that simple thought which disappears in the millions of other thoughts.

Revival Sanctuary was just a thought for me back in 2017. I didn't realise then how impactful and valued it could and would become to so many including to me.

I had just started out on my self-employment journey. I was lost. I tried networking. Met some lovely people, but nothing excited me. I didn't feel a real connection with any of them and the ones I did connect with were talkers, not action takers. It was frustrating.

I'd always worked in the corporate world from leaving school at 16 right up until I was 46 years old. Not a day without working for someone else or in a team of some sort or ever being out of work. That regular pay check came for 30 years solid and it was my crutch.

When you leave this kind of security, yes, it's exciting but it's also terrifying to lose a regular income especially with the realisation that NOW you'll have to figure out a way to make your own money. A million questions swirl in your mind, the biggest one being... HOW am I going to convince someone to buy my service?I had started my events business in 2015 but the first couple of years were spent building websites, experimenting with various types of events i.e. live music, corporate, workshops etc. I'd had a real buzz when doing it in corporate but I just wasn't making any real money even two years in. I needed help. I needed a team of good people around me to work together.

After networking my socks off, I still didn't feel I had found my people. I realised in 2017 that if I wanted what I was looking for, I'd have to create it myself. Again, the self-doubt crept in. There are so many out there, why would people want to sign up to mine?

I set the plan in motion. I did the research, the groundwork, I learned fast how to build my own website that could take payments. I pushed it out there with the message I had looked for myself for so long, COLLABORATION over COMPETITION. Would other women feel like this? Would they have experienced the incessant jealousy, bitchyness and cut-throat world that corporate constantly spits out at you? We'll see I thought.

Two years on. over 200 members have joined us, over 20 nationalities, 15 networking locations, a global business magazine, two trademarks, two published books with a third on the way. Over 70 Author opportunities created, two business retreats and so much more on the way....

NEVER GIVE UP ON YOUR DREAMS...

ALISON BLANEY-WOMBWELL

Founder
CHASING RAINBOWS /
I AM HER VOICE AUTISM JOURNEY

Iamhervoice.co.uk
alison@iamhervoice.co.uk

CHAPTER 1

Little Girl Lost - On the Other Side

July 2019 - the month and year that will forever stay with me. It was when my whole life changed. I had just received a diagnosis of Autism. I was thirty-four years old.

At a time when I should have felt relieved and at peace finally understanding who I was, I did not, in fact, I felt incredibly low. I felt like everything that I thought I was, was a lie. It was like someone had said, you are autistic now, you can take your mask off, you can be yourself. I did not know how to be myself.

Throughout my life I had struggled silently.

I often found it difficult to understand other people, often shutting down when I needed to socially interact with others for long periods. Autism wasn't new to me; I knew about the condition inside out. I had two children, ironically both girls, with a diagnosis. I had always known there was something different about me. When I say different, I mean I had always struggled with my mental health and in social situations. I had become so good at 'masking' all my life that I felt like my life was just one big act.

In order to maintain friendships, I thought I had to please them and I had felt that I had to constantly apologise - by doing this I felt I didn't stand out. I had become an expert at masking my difficulties. Often the difficulties that others could see, more so when I was younger, would be seen as reckless and somewhat impulsive.

When we think of impulsive behaviours, we think of going on a scary theme park ride when we are genuinely terrified. It could be buying a scratch card when you are in your local shop and you notice the amount you could win, so you buy it without thinking. Now I want you to think of a person who cannot stop being impulsive, spending money that they know they couldn't pay back, debt mounting and completely spiralling out of control.

I had consistently managed for fifteen years to live like this.

Every time something happened, especially in situations where I felt I had no control I would spend money or I would do something without thinking. Often the conclusion would be that I would end up in situations that I had no control over.

In 2019 I not only found that I had Autism but I also had ADHD. I knew quite a lot about this condition, mostly how it affected children, especially boys, but not adults. Little did I know that actually my over active mind and constantly bored brain was only just a small part of this misunderstood condition. Receiving a dual diagnosis literally changed my life. I had waited so long to know why I thought the way that I did and I needed answers for so many behaviours that I never received the correct support to deal with it.

In fact, after getting my diagnosis, I was bitter, I was angry. I could not understand why it had taken so long for people to realise that everything that I had struggled with and everything that I could have actually achieved could have been supported and it could have been accomplished if I had let people understand the real me.

It's ironic really that in the same year that I was diagnosed with a condition that I had masked for so long, I actually achieved something amazing and something that I was actually interested in for the first time in my life. At the start of last year, I actually felt like I was on top of the world. I had not long since started a new job role, I was learning more about myself and understanding how best to support my mental health for the first time in my life.

Who was I kidding?

Less than six months later I broke down, my mental health was probably at its lowest and for someone who had battled anorexia and anxiety disorder previously I needed a break, I needed support, the same support for myself that I had always tried to give others.

Isn't it strange though when you think that, at that time I should have realised that I needed a break and I needed to slow down. Instead, that ADHD brain of mine (pre-treatment and support) decided to think of new ideas for me to stop being bored. I did something that actually in hindsight most people would have thought, at the time, I shouldn't and that I should have been slowing down. I felt like I had to try and succeed at something.

Boy, am I glad I did try!

You see people don't realise that I had spent a lifetime of starting new ventures and getting bored, and then I would move onto the next interesting thing in my mind. I knew in the back of my mind what I wanted to do.

I wanted to set up my own support and training service to help families, children and adults understand that they are not alone. I had first-hand experience of feeling like that, for such a long time. I was also incredibly passionate about my training, I had written all my own training workshops, based on personal experience.

The ironic thing is even though I have a brain that is always going for the next best thing, writing workshops is a passion of mine. I can easily hyper-focus when I am writing. I guess it is an escapism for me.

Setting up on my own and becoming self-employed was both terrifying and exciting at the same time.

I was quickly given a number of exciting opportunities even from the start. I was commissioned to deliver training immediately to help both families and professionals understand girls on the spectrum. At the same time, I was hitting many personal hurdles and it wasn't until the end of 2019 after my ADHD was finally properly diagnosed and was being treated I realised what I was capable of.

I remember what it felt like to be me finally after all this time. It was like that accelerator pedal had finally come with a brake and I knew when to use it. The constant motor feeling was slowing down. This had amazing results for my business and personally. I was able to move forward and pick my clients, deciding which ones would benefit from my support and coaching.

I had moved all of my training online by Spring 2020, that in itself was something I never believed I could achieve. I now have clients from across the UK and some families are from different continents.

My workshop list has increased and I now have over ten self-written workshops which are being commissioned by private psychologists and professionals across the country.

I genuinely love what I do, and if helping to support a child or adult through coaching and 1:1 sessions, and by educating people through my workshops, I can make a difference, then that right there is my job satisfaction.

I have children who one day may need extra support when I am not there. My job as a parent, and an adult with the same conditions as them, is to educate those care workers, social workers, health workers and others around them so that they can understand how the conditions affect them. I know that I will never be able to have a normal job, but who defines what a normal job is?

I also know that the best decision I ever made was going self-employed and setting up Chasing Rainbows. It allows me to be in control of what I do. It allows me to protect my mental and physical health and most importantly it allows me to be me. When setting up a business you have to overcome many hurdles before you find your feet. I've learnt more from my past and my mistakes, which has actually helped me with my business and as a person. That is my motivation and drive for the future of Chasing Rainbows.

You have to experience a few storms before a rainbow appears and I'm so happy and fortunate that the rainbow is staying with me. The difference is now I can handle the storms.

ANDREA GILLARD

Interior Designer
ANDREA GILLARD DESIGN

andreagillarddesign.com
andrea@andreagillard.com

CHAPTER 2

Finding My Sanctuary

Have you ever walked into a room and felt instantly at ease? Or, conversely, entered a space and suddenly experienced a shiver up your spine leaving you feeling cold and alone? These feelings are directly evoked by the light quality and décor, and, I don't know about you but, I'd preferably not have the latter experience. Knowing how to create the right ambience takes skill and knowledge.

My journey into business has been rather unconventional but, looking back, was something I was always destined to do.

I've always looked back on my childhood as being a happy one, which it was, but on reflection it wasn't one of defined, inspirational role models; my mom was a stay-at-home-mum, until she got a Saturday job at the brand-new Asda, when I was about 7 years old. Whilst she was gone, my older brother and I sat and watched the Saturday morning cartoons and 'Swap Shop' or played in the garden until she came home.

My dad had taken a particularly hard career route by studying for his degree whilst being a young parent and working full-time. We'd never had any money; as my parents couldn't afford to take us into cafes, whenever we 'went to town' (going into Sheffield) on Saturdays (shops didn't open on Sundays in my day!), they would pack up sandwiches and a flask of coffee for us which, no matter how cold the weather, we'd partake of whilst sat on the benches in the Peace Gardens – oh, the days of me shivering with the wind whistling round my ears aren't particularly rosy, I can tell you!

In retrospect it would appear this frugality must have subliminally engrained itself into my persona as it wasn't until meeting my husband, Iain, that I'd ever gone into a coffee shop simply to 'pass the time' or 'treat' myself to a 'posh coffee'. In fact, I remember the first time I ever ventured into a Costa I looked desperately up and down the board, having no idea what all the different variations were and simply, pathetically pleaded with the Barista, "I'd just like a normal coffee, please. Do you do those?" He smiled (probably to understandably later laugh at my expense with his colleagues!) and got me an Americano; a type I never touch now I've found the decaf, coconut milk, hazelnut latte!

The lack of funds whilst growing up shaped my life in that I was always grateful for the things I did have, so I really looked after and cherished them. I used to keep my bedroom immaculate and ensure my 'treasures' were as aesthetically placed as possible so I could fully indulge in my own tranquil space. This was equally important as my dad has an explosive temper and I would shut myself in my little box-room, sit on the floor, with my back against my bed and feet against my door, so no-one could get in.

It's amazing the survival tricks you learn at such a young age. My dad had never physically hit any of us, but I hated being around when he went into one of his volcanic eruptions!

I would spend hours in my room, playing with my dolls. I converted two shelves in my wardrobe to develop a bijou apartment for my Sindys and Barbies, even designing a 'glass lift', years before I'd ever seen one, by using a single-rose delivery tube and cutting out a hole between 'floors' (shelves), just so they had actual access to the next floor, to utilise the space to its full potential.

Totally immersing myself in this little world created the foundations for my spatial and aesthetic planning abilities. Spending hours painstakingly moving the furniture around to create zones but ensuring an easy flow from one area to another was key. I'd ensure there were vignettes prepared each evening before closing the doors and putting them to bed.

These traits of surrounding myself in tranquillity and spatial flow followed me into my first two marriages and helped me to retain some sort of stability in my mental health. Both ex-husbands were abusive and controlling in different ways, so my survival mode presented itself in me developing a home where I was cushioned by pleasing settings, textures and calming colours; this was the one and only aspect of my environment I could control.

On meeting Iain, I have found my soulmate and dream-sharer. He more than meets me halfway in tasks around the home and I'm given the freedom and space to grow and flourish that I'd never had the privilege of at any point before in my life. He loves me totally, body and soul, and it's wholly reciprocated.

We share the same love of design. He's a bench-joiner by trade and has worked on prestigious projects within Harrods and handmade bespoke display cabinetry for Montblanc and Dunhill. He is the Mr. Darcy to my Miss Bennett!

We're both massively into personal development. However, slowly the truth of me never allowing myself to escape the shackles of 'being a wife', from my past relationships and my mom's own stance in my parents' marriage, began to reveal itself.

This eye-opener began to emerge in 2013. I remember sitting in a workshop run by Claire Cahill (Accendo Coaching) and being asked, "What are your goals?" I immediately burst into tears and sobbed, "I don't have any. I'm just the glue that holds everyone together." Wife, mother, daughter, full-time employee. Everything I'd ever wanted to do, or places I wanted to go, came second (or third, or fourth) to whatever anyone else wanted to do! Can you hear those tiny violins!

Iain was devasted as he'd never realised that I'd kow-towed to everyone else's wants and desires. However, I'm not a victim, the fault is mine, as I'd not spoken up and advertised my own dreams.

Looking back, I see that one of the reasons my mom has eternally forgiven my dad for his anger outbursts is because of how he loves to help people. I remember him being awake for 36 hours, mending a friend's car and then pack-ing our own car and caravan to drive my mom, me and my best friend down to Cornwall for our holiday. In retrospect, this was a wholly irresponsible and dangerous thing to do; our family friends had more than ample disposable income and could have easily afforded to take their car to a garage, but my dad loves to be everyone's saviour; it's what makes him tick, but it's also his Achilles heel, as he seems to strug-gle when people are able to cope without him. I believe he has abandonment issues due to his dad leaving him and his older siblings, without trace, when he was three.

Fast forward three years and I had embarked on a Napoleon Hill, 'Think and Grow Rich' Mindset workshop, run by my own wonderful husband, and, being the con-scientious student I am (ahem!), I was completing my assigned homework of reading a chapter of the book, on the bus, the following morning when I suddenly burst into tears. There's a theme going on here, isn't there!? However, the difference this time was that the tears were a 'Eureka' moment of 'I know what it is I'm meant to do! I'm meant to be a designer!'

This was a complete turning point for me and instantly I knew 'my place' in the world and how everything that had ever interested me since being a child would be my own vocation and legacy. Where I would differ from my dad, is that I wouldn't "give a man a fish and feed him for a day," making them eternally dependent on me, I would "teach a man to fish and feed him for life;" by creating someone's sanctuary in their world they would be able to flourish in their own soothing space, totally unhindered by dysfunctional areas, allowing their dreams and goals to flourish, unhindered in serene surroundings.

I never take the easy route, so my first ever professional undertaking was to be no different. To build my portfolio, I offered to fully re-design a local restaurant for free. The prerequisite was that the new owners would promote me on their website and in any interviews they undertook. I took an orange, purple and red monstrosity, that locals protested against there being another restaurant in its place, into a serene and tranquil fine-dining experience that the same locals subsequently flocked to, and even received plaudits in 'The Times' for its "fine tranquil décor".

I project managed every single aspect, from design of the exterior, interior, all fittings, fixtures and furniture, including commissioning my bespoke talking-piece bar, and negotiation with HSE; all this to have NO advertisement whatsoever! Lesson number one learnt, NEVER do anything for free, know your worth and make sure you get it.

I didn't take this to heart, it's all part of the steep learning curve and I believe in karma! I rose above it, having now educated myself in resilience and knowing my self-worth so will never undersell myself again. If you want to find Sanctuary in *Your* World, look no further than me.

ANNA GOODWIN

Accountant / Mentor
ANNA GOODWIN ACCOUNTANCY LTD

Annagoodwinaccountancy.co.uk
anna@annagoodwinaccountancy.co.uk

CHAPTER 3

When Your Life Path Takes
An Unusual Turn

I suffered with school phobia. As an 8-year-old sitting in my maths class, I felt scared and overwhelmed and knew that asking a question wouldn't help as I wouldn't understand the answer. Looking back on these times as an adult, I recognise that the teacher was a bully, but of course I didn't then.

After finishing my A levels, I decided not to go to university and instead started to look for work. I think, at this point, my mum despaired of me and paid for me to go to the Career Analysts in London. This was a turning point for me! Imagine my shock when I was told I should work as an accountant or in tax. "But what about my maths?" I asked. She replied, "It's ok, the main thing is your attention to detail and checking".

I'm naturally cautious so I started off by undertaking a one-year Financial Course in Accounting at Wolverhampton University. What a shock to the system after studying French, German and English A levels! I stayed behind after most classes asking questions, especially the Economics and Statistics! I had gained confidence by going to the Career Analysts and therefore felt able to ask questions. Imagine my delight when I got a First in Statistics! It felt as though I was leaving behind my childhood trauma. From then on, I have had a firm belief that there are no stupid questions and always encourage clients to ask – otherwise how can you learn?

I went on to study a degree specialising in Finance and then sat my professional exams when I worked in Birmingham. Those nine years helped me to understand the basics of finance, as well as how to interact as a team member and work with clients. It was such a useful time for me as I learnt a lot from the other members of staff, both in how to be as efficient as possible at work and how to get the best out of the clients.

In 1997 I decided to move to London to use my French. I lived in France when I was five years old and after chatting away to a Swiss guy on holiday, I decided I wanted to use my French at work. What a change London was; leaving family and friends behind, working somewhere completely different and frequently in French! It even involved travelling to France.

Working in France was a fantastic experience both personally and for my business skills. I carried out one-day audits of universities and Chambers of Commerce to check that they had used their European Commission grants correctly. I grew into myself and finally grew up. Having to get eleven French people to do what you want them to do in a meeting does that for you! Also travelling on my own around France – whether by train, plane or in a car – was a great experience and taught me to become independent and focused on where I was going.

After working in London and France for 6.5 years I decided to move back home. I felt burnt out – in London you work hard and play hard! I got a job working for a small accountancy firm but there was a lot of audit work. Too boring for me so I decided to leave.

It's funny how opportunities arise, though, as soon as you decide to leave something behind. Before I left, one of the clients asked the Partner if I could continue preparing her monthly management accounts. She said, "I can understand Anna". All the other staff members were posh!

That was the start of my business. With only one client, I knew I would need more income so I started working as an accountant for a small sound and lighting company.

I had to give up this employed work once my self-employed work took off. There are only so many emails and calls you can answer in your lunch hour! It was a steep learning curve being fully self-employed. I was used to having the support of people at work and having someone to ask. The challenges I faced, and in many ways I continue to face, are:

- Finding the right staff to support me. I have struggled with this in every area of running my business, be it bookkeeping, accountancy, administration or marketing. As a small business owner, you don't have enough work to employ someone full time but there is too much to do yourself! However, if you find the perfect person for that work, they become a life saver!

- Managing my time. Of course, the above will have impacted on this. Also, I can get distracted by emails coming in or clients phoning. If I know people are stuck and I can help, I tend to want to do it straight away.

- Juggling business development and work. It's always a struggle to put as much energy and focus onto business development as paid work. I tend to find that one or the other will suffer as I have a spurt of energy and focus on one of these areas.

When I first started working for myself, I worked as a conventional accountant, but things changed fundamentally when my friend Ruth, who was also an accountant, died of cancer in 2013. People had always said to me you ought to write a book but I always discounted it. What on earth would I write about? Not long after my friend's death, a mind map of my first book, 'Accountants Don't Bite' came to me. This was published in 2014 and was a guide for business owners covering what to ask an accountant and why you need one.

Basically, the book encourages people to make the best use of their accountant and shows them how to build a better relationship. This book was a milestone for me and it was important that the message was clear and something close to my heart. A good relationship with your accountant is worth its weight in gold and business owners need to ensure that their accountant is the right fit for them.

In 2014 I also organised my first Empowerment event with all of the profits going to Compton Hospice, where Ruth died. Her last text to me was that, "This place is awesome!" This event was an opportunity for people to showcase their businesses. Everyone had a great time, which was the most important thing, but also, there was a lot of networking that took place that day and I was proud of this celebration of Ruth's life. The following year I put on a similar event, this time in aid of Cystic Fibrosis, which my nephew has; he is thirty years old this year.

Over the next few years, I published three of Anna's Simple Accounting Guides and my last book, 'Your Business Your Numbers'. Once I started writing, I couldn't stop! All of these books are aimed at helping people in an easy to understand, jargon-free way. This is another priority for me as I believe that if you can't understand your business numbers, how can you be successful in running your business?

The future shines bright as I believe that, after 16 years of working for myself, I now know me. I know my likes and dislikes. I know that I make a difference to people and their businesses. I know my ideal client, and I know who I can call upon in my business support network.

Fundamentally, I like helping people to grow, so one of the areas I'm focusing on is increasing the mentoring side of my business. Also, I provide online courses on Managing Personal Finances and Finance for Non-Financial Managers and I would like to get these out there as I am a firm believer that if you can manage your personal finances, you can manage your business finances and your stress levels come right down.

An area I've enjoyed over the last few years is training – both face to face and virtually – and I would like to do more of this.

For the last thirty years I have worked with small businesses and I have learnt a lot about how they work and the difficulties they face. From both my personal experience and working with others, my advice is:

- Do something you love
- Do it your way
- Ask for help
- Fit in time for you

I have grown a lot compared with the fearful eight-year-old girl. However, this experience instilled in me a desire to help people without bullying them and without judgement. Anyone with the right support can understand their financial figures and use them to develop their business and I'm here to help them to do exactly that!

ARAH PERRETT

Business Owner
ARAH PERRETT CONSULTANCY LTD

Arahperrett.co.uk
hello@arahperrett.co.uk

CHAPTER 4

Beginning

My name is Arah Perrett – pronounced like Sarah but without the S. As I write this, I am 58 years old, live in Gloucestershire and am as contented as I have ever been in my life. But hey, I am getting ahead of myself. I'll start at the beginning.

Growing up, I lived with my parents, younger brother and sister in a rather deprived part of London. It is a very different, gentrified neighbourhood now with homes that command high prices.

My childhood memories are rather patchy. When I talk to other people about their memories, they string events together and share a detailed story about what happened, almost as if they were describing a movie. My memories have never been like that. I experience them more as sensory stills that don't always connect to anything else.

So, what do I remember? My parents were hopelessly mismatched. Dad was an outgoing, handsome man with a sharp intellect that he sometimes used as a weapon. He was also a functioning alcoholic and compulsive gambler. Mum was an intelligent, complex woman who 'suffered with her nerves'. This combination led to a turbulent family life that rode the highs and lows of their co–dependent relationship. To an outsider this must sound awful and my family was known to social services during those years. And yet, within the turbulence there were oases of peace and many of my memories are wonderful.

It was important to my mum that her three children escape the poverty trap that she had fallen into. In many ways she was ahead of her time. I suspect that if she were born today, with more opportunities available to her, her life would have been very different. She taught me to read before I went to school and instilled a love of learning and education that I have to this day. I was a bookish, imaginative child who read voraciously, and had a precocious love of language. This is possibly what drew me to the attention of my primary school headmistress. Mrs. Bishop helped me to get into a good City of London Grammar School. This would never have happened without her intervention. I count this as the first big break that I had in my life. I received an education that has stood me in good stead. This is also an example of a certain knack that I have to attract the right people into my life at the right time, to the mutual benefit of all concerned.

Regardless of my love for mum, I left home at 16 and married young. In retrospect this was probably a means to escape. I had my first son at 18.

My twenties were a tough, painful decade. Mum died of cancer, followed two years later, suddenly, by my 23-year-old brother. My father was in the grip of early onset dementia. There is that saying, 'what doesn't kill you makes you stronger', a cliché, but it is also true. On the other hand, my gorgeous second son was born and my career began to take off.

I was working in a bank and passed my financial planning exams, crucial to my advancement, within days of my brother's funeral. I was both grieving and determined to go on for myself and for my family, alive and dead. There was also a new, positive influence in my life; a manager joined my branch and recommended that I train to become a Financial Adviser. Recent experiences had drained my confidence and I hadn't considered that I was good enough to be promoted. The difference it makes when someone declares that they believe in you! Her mentorship was pivotal.

During my thirties, I discovered Stephen Covey's amazing book, The 7 Habits of Highly Effective People. Personal development is an obsession of mine, fuelled by my mum's desire for me to succeed. This book became my bible; I lived and breathed what I learned. This included taking full responsibility for my life and not using a difficult start as a reason not to get ahead.

Following the habits helped me to achieve a series of rapid promotions, culminating in a Senior Manager role responsible for generating millions of pounds of new business. It was during this period that I discovered my talent for, and love of, developing people. I gained a reputation for turning around the performance of struggling individuals and businesses. I was in my element and this is one of the happiest times in my employed working career. So, my professional life was good. This wasn't, however, matched by other areas in my life. The relationship with my husband began to break down and our 20-year marriage ended. We had married young and were now different people who had little in common. We separated amicably and still have a good, though distant relationship.

At 40 I moved away from management. I had been made redundant from a job that I didn't enjoy and was exhausted by the process of constantly pushing to achieve increasingly outrageous sales targets. I read a book called 'What Colour is Your Parachute' and would recommend this to anyone who is considering a career change. That and my natural inclination led me to my first full time training role. I seriously flirted with the idea of starting a business at this point. However, as a single parent, I felt the heavy weight of responsibility to provide a stable home with a regular income for my sons, 'the beautiful boys'. I tucked the idea away as something that I could always do later, although I didn't really see how it could happen.

In February 2017, I was 55 and at home recovering from an asthma flare up. Bored and listless, I cast around for something to do. My mind wandered back to a course I had attended the previous November where the leader had referred to a film called The Secret. With an afternoon stretching ahead of me, I decided to rent the film on Amazon. What I saw blew my mind and I went on to devour the accompanying book. I was entranced by some of the concepts: 'we are what we think about', the law of attraction, our capacity to achieve the seemingly impossible if we allow ourselves to entertain the idea that everything is possible. I made the decision that day to say Yes to opportunities that came my way, however, scary. It was like putting on my hiking boots to go on a new expedition. The trip has been both internal and external and I suspect I will be on it for the rest of my days.

Since then my life has changed almost beyond recognition. I have moved home, twice, and now live in the Cotswolds with my partner. In many ways I am a changed individual. I embrace meditation, yoga and my own spirituality. I work just as much on being a better person as I do to improve my external situation. My relationships have benefited, while there are also some that I have consciously let go. I made the leap from a secure employed role to own a business in the area that I love.

It used to bother me that I hadn't been more proactive and made some of these changes sooner. However, I have come to realise that I needed to acquire a level of emotional maturity that wasn't available to the younger Arah. I am right where I should be.

If you want to start a business, my advice is simple:

- *Seek expert advice* - I invested in a training programme for fledgling entrepreneurs. The instruction and support I received were invaluable. I also worked with a business coach in my first year.

- *Collaborate as soon as possible* – it is difficult to scale up any business without help.

- *Get a good accountant* – I procrastinated about this for a long time which made preparing for my first set of accounts a real headache.

It is also never too late to start a business; if you feel you have something to offer, do it.

I train, coach, consult and nag clients to help them be the best that they possibly can be in their professional and personal lives. Why do I do it? That's easy; I want to be a Mrs. Bishop in other people's lives – the right person at the right time that makes the difference.

Today I am at the beginning of the rest of my life. There are many things that I still want to achieve. I want to grow my business into an award-winning company with a £1,000,000 turnover and I would love to own a country cottage retreat. The best thing of all is that I know I can, because everything is possible.

Thank you to all of the people in my life who have made a difference.

GABRIELLE ANYA RAFELLO

Writer | Mentor | Facilitator |
Specialist in Vibrational Medicine
Director of THE KOORANA CENTRE and
THE KOORANA FOUNDATION
Creating Spaces Where People Thrive

Gabrielleanyarafello.com
gabrielle@gabrielleanyarafello.com

Thekooranacentre.com
info@thekooranacentre.com

CHAPTER 5

Angels On My Side

As one who became aware of a spiritual path many years ago, I believe we plan much of this life long before we arrive here. Glancing back, I realise that each experience was perfect but may not have made much sense at the time. The main theme seems to have been growing in confidence and reawakening a power, then holding space for other women to do the same.

If I am honest it was my resistance to change that created pain, I did as much as I could to try to 'fit in'. Through adversity we certainly discover our greatest gifts and for me those were self-acceptance and resilience, which were destined to arrive eventually. My advice for that younger Gabrielle would be to stress less, let go more and not take everything so seriously. I have often learnt the hard way, but genuinely believe that when we trust in life it responds wholeheartedly, showing us the direction. Sometimes that arrives in a subtle way. I have been blessed with many signs to guide me and feel I have always had angels on my side.

With a varied career spanning 33 years, I enjoyed time in fashion and retail, and in education. I have worked in businesses and for charities. I am not sure that anyone would want to employ me now, I love to do things my way!

There are many threads woven into my story and I believe I have now reached a stage where I can appreciate each one. My love of colour and pattern has remained consistent and I began my working life in trend prediction at the tender age of 18, making vision boards for well-known fashion companies in London. Now I share retreats where vision boards lead people safely into their creative process. I love working with women who are awakening to their gifts and doing the best to honour their sensitivity.

I have always been an empath. The qualities I embraced led me into the path of healing and developing my own modality. At home I feel blessed to enjoy a piece of land with ancient trees and a wild grassy meadow where I try to spend time each day. It is a sacred space that always seems to hold me. The way that environments support our health and wellbeing is a subject close to my heart.

Today I am a professional mentor and facilitator with my own wellbeing centre. It has taken 14 years to carve that path and reach the growing audience I feel blessed to serve. I teach vibrational medicine and love making things with my hands. What guided me into this line of work? That is an interesting question. I felt there was a need to create a safe space where people could be open and discover the gifts they have.

At college I studied textile design and created natural dyes using flowers, vegetables, roots and bark. I learnt to knit, to spin and to weave, and to share my stories, much like my ancestors would have done. I felt proud of my lineage, Scottish on my mother's side.

I remember my art teacher once said in a somewhat dismissive tone "you will never make it to art college" and I set out to prove him wrong. There has always been a fiery spark within me. I can be determined and stubborn when I need. I wanted to give up numerous times, but somehow always found what was necessary to carry on. Taking the easy way through life never really appealed.

One of my earliest memories was on sports day back in primary school, aged 7 and being part of a relay. The girl before me dropped the baton and as a team we lost valuable seconds in our lead as I went back to pick it up. The other teams raced forward, and we dropped far behind. I remember this surreal experience where time stood still and my energy lifted completely out of my body, like I was in a dream. I had a knowing we would recover and win and a vision of holding the trophy. As my spirit dropped back into my physical legs, which seemed to almost gallop on before me, the girl ahead in my team grabbed the baton from my hand and flew towards the finishing line. It was great to be part of a winning team! I have always been rather petite in size and could never be described as 'sporty', but the focus and determination I felt that day has never really left me.

I have always loved children and when my youngest was born things really started to intensify, I knew the moment he arrived that he was part of my Soul family. My interest in personal development began and I trained in many therapies. Any free time I had was spent in like-minded company and getting to know myself in a whole new way.

Learning to let go was a consistent theme which repeated itself frequently and the lessons came in thick and fast with little warning. I was on an accelerated path where feelings of deep sadness would often arrive as I rapidly outgrew situations and I found that somewhat isolating. Feeling secure as we awaken is not always easy and I have known many to experience their earlier growth in this way. Staying grounded was the safest option, especially as I began to teach, and I felt a growing desire to keep others safe too. Being true to myself was also a big lesson and I needed to find ways to express myself more clearly. It became important for me to create spaces where people could relax and speak openly without fear of being judged in any way.

I opened the Koorana Centre in 2012 which is a space for health and wellbeing. 'Koorana' is an aboriginal term, which means 'to bring forward the children' and I also run a not-for-profit foundation which supports families too.

The plan for Koorana arrived during a week-long retreat where I received an interesting reading. The medium told me I would soon be working in an old church with red walls and black beams and the congregation would be my clients! What a surprise that was to hear and it came in almost immediately. For some reason I did not focus on the 'how', I just knew it would happen. I put my retail business on the market and managed to sell it in the recession.

I needed faith for this new mission and looking back there were many times this choice could have scared me. But something very real, which I find hard to explain, kept moving me forward in the right direction. Soon, the bond between me and that space could not be broken. During the three-month restoration, that beautiful Victorian chapel experienced a powerful transformation and on one occasion I felt that in my body so profoundly. I walked in one day to see the floor ripped out, it was rotten. My stomach dropped and began to churn. I realised the connection.

Running a centre has taught me far more than I ever thought possible and it took time to build a solid platform. I learnt to create and maintain boundaries and develop greater business sense, which was not always easy. My work often requires a regular change in frequency and walking between layers of reality that often remain unseen. I gave it everything. The opportunities were immense, and Spirit sent many who would help me. I was able to travel to new countries, learn new skills and bring those back for my community, making the space a unique sanctuary for many to enjoy.

My advice for others with a similar dream is to be true to their heart and follow its guidance. When we feel aligned to our vision we just need to keep going and trust our break will come. The power of intention is an incredible thing and sets in motion so much of what we experience now and in the future. With strong belief and a healthy form of exchange we can achieve what we set out to do, but should not be surprised if the plan changes, that is often how we learn. I realised many years ago there is also a Divine plan and what we offer must align with all that is needed for the greater good.

I hope that my space will continue to grow. I love being part of a community and having opportunities to collaborate with others. I feel our world is changing, and I hope the next generation will inherit something that is of great value, even more beautiful, magical and peaceful. It is such a privilege to be part of the movement that will bring that in.

GAVIN JAMES

BEYOND THE ARC

Beyondthearc.com

CHAPTER 6

Ask For What You Want

"I put a lot of love in, and I want a lot of love back".

That's the mantra I chose to guide my journey, as I took a leap of faith into a new business 15 years ago. As a communications and customer experience consultant, it has been the true North on my compass. This mantra reminds me who I am, helps me realign when needed, and stay in tune with my intuition to manifest what I want.

But I'm getting ahead of myself. Like many creative self-employed people, my journey, and that mantra, were sparked by painful lessons I was determined never to repeat, and a deep knowing that I have superpowers that will be valuable to others.

Moments of truth

Two back-to-back work experiences shaped the professional I am today.

20 years ago, I worked at Microsoft leading writing and design teams. Technology was the focus, not the users, and I wanted to change that. I did extensive research to innovate how we might make products easier and more fun to learn and use. After presenting to leadership, my

boss (who had been at the company for decades) told me, "This is really cool. But it's 5 years ahead of its time. No one is ready for it yet".

Right then I decided: I KNOW this is important, and I know it's going to be a thing – and that's where I'm headed.

Fast forward to 2020. Creating empathetic customer experiences is now one of the most talked about things in business. It's very validating, and thankfully, it keeps me busy.

My mantra, however, was sparked by harder knocks. At Microsoft, endless long hours and sweat were rewarded with a rollercoaster of re-orgs, being tossed around and unappreciated. Management was more about ego and empire, than valuing great work.

So, I left and helped launch a tech start-up. More long hours and sweat, but I thrived in the challenges. However, eventually the founder's ego took precedence over good sense. I tried to convince him and others that the complex software was too hard to learn and use, but it fell on deaf ears. Instead they scapegoated me, saying I was a bad trainer if people couldn't understand the product. I felt betrayed.

What I regret more is that I got defensive. I tried to explain myself as if I had actually done wrong, when instead I should have owned my worth, and given them the choice words they deserved about where to shove their job.

A phoenix rising from the ashes

I decided to go it on my own. When I launched my consultancy in 2005, I needed a grounding principle to cleanse away those bitter experiences. Enter my mantra: "I put a lot of love in, and I want a lot of love back". This intention would guide how I'm treated, the kind of clients and work I attract, how I'm compensated, and more.

I'm a rare bird in my industry. Usually one person writes, another designs, and a third infuses human factors perspective on what influences behaviours, attitudes, and actions. My expertise spans all three because I believe they are essential all together for creating communications that help people connect in meaningful ways.

By offering all three services in one person, I save clients time, money and frustration, while making their business shine. That helps reinforce that my expertise and efforts are well worth whatever they pay me – so money could be a non-issue.

I also deliver value by speaking my truth. My goal is to help clients elevate their game and do right by their customers. Sometimes that means challenging the way they've always done things, or the direction they think they need, when it may not be in their best interest. Ultimately, people respect that, so don't be afraid to have a voice!

Stretching my wings

I found joy in many creative challenges across a wide range of marketing communications, with clients in healthcare, real estate, an architect, even a movie producer. Then in 2007, I collaborated with someone who would change the trajectory of my work to this day.

Steven represented the creativity, respect, brilliance, and fun I wanted in my work, and when a cool opportunity came his way, he asked for my help. Together, we launched a communications project that grew into what is now a 13-year relationship with a Top 5 bank. Between my independent consulting and working part-time with his agency (Beyond the Arc), my dance card was packed.

But don't think it was all lollipops and roses. My work was an escape. Through all of this, I was fielding a tumultuous marriage in Seattle, living half-frozen in an old rental house, and supporting us both when he went back to school. Daily life was crap unless I was immersed in my work or digging in my garden.

Eventually I gave myself permission to leave -- my marriage and Seattle -- and returned to San Francisco. In 2013, I felt ready for a new challenge. It appeared soon after, when I was asked to join the agency full-time. This transition meant we could take on bigger, more strategically important creative projects, and I could grow to my own next level.

It was a brilliant move that's given me the best of many worlds. I have the freedom of an independent consultant, with the security of a salary and bennies. I work with industry leading clients, constantly expanding my knowledge and skills. And, I am blessed to partner with amazingly bright, loving people. It's the ultimate manifestation of my mantra, and I never stop being grateful.

Empowering my journey going forward

A hard lesson learned is that if I don't live by Design, I will live by Default (And that's usually not good). So, I've also been designing my life with more time for travel and personal creative passions.

Instead of focusing on things, I focus on how I want to FEEL – then I ask the Universe to help me bring it, in 'any way possible'. I get specific about the Feeling, yet stay open about how it might manifest, because it often comes in ways I never would have imagined.

A powerful example is this book. I had been wanting to feel "excited and inspired", open to any person, place, or experience that would fill me with that feeling. While networking on LinkedIn to connect with empowering women, I met Sharon Brown, the heart and soul of this book, and the founder of the Revival Sanctuary. Instantly that name resonated with me. Soon I had joined her community of women entrepreneurs and was contributing my story to her next book! Talk about feeling excited and inspired!

Words to live by

Long ago, a friend told me, "Once you know what you really want, it's already there". Perfect advice that has proven true over and over in my life. So, I'll end with a little advice of my own and hope it sparks ideas for others.

- **Protection.** Speak your truth and set healthy boundaries, especially for your worth, so you don't give away value for nothing. Also, pay close attention to your earliest communications with people, and trust your intuition about it. They are showing you what it will be like to deal with them over time, good or bad.

- **Manifestation.** Create a clear vision of how you want to FEEL. That feeling can apply to the work you do, your clients, how you get compensated, etc. The more you connect with your desired feeling, the more energy you will generate to attract that to you.

- **Perseverance.** You CAN do this. It just takes willingness and practice to step into your new self. And you are never alone. Every one of us has been called to take those steps toward becoming something more, something better – to grow into the best expression of ourselves; and you will too.

GILL WHITTY-COLLINS

Author of WHY MEN WIN AT WORK
Consultant | Keynote Speaker | Coach

gillwhittycollins.com
gill.whittycollins@gmail.com

CHAPTER 7

The Penny Drop Moment

'd love to be able to start my story by saying I'm from Liverpool. My entire family was born there – mum, dad, sisters, cousins, everyone – but my parents moved house just before I came along in 1970 so I was born in Warrington General Hospital. I don't think I have ever quite forgiven them for me not being a legitimate Scouser.

I was the third of three daughters and the doctor who delivered me told my dad that I was a boy. He was so excited and I think he refused to accept that I wasn't his son – he brought me up to support Liverpool FC and to play football and pool. He was quite the 'femanist' in fact, he and my mum taught all of their girls from the start that we were as intelligent and capable as any boy. For many years it never really occurred to me to question whether I was as good as or equal to a man. It helped that I went to mixed schools where, thanks to a combination of sufficient intelligence and being famously well organised, I was usually top of the class or close to it.

I was also extremely focused and hard-working, a classic 'girly swot' in the words of my schoolmates. Looking back this was in part due to the 'curse of perfectionism' that many girls experience at school, but it was more because

I knew from a very early age that I didn't want to spend the rest of my life in Warrington, or even in the UK.

I fell in love with France and the French language while on a camping holiday in Brittany at the grand age of 5 with my family. I loved the baguettes, the croissants, the Nutella, the hypermarkets, the weather, the language – everything. We went on holiday to France virtually every summer after that, exploring the Atlantic and Mediterranean coast and graduating from tent to caravan to the luxury of mobile homes. These were the happiest holidays of my life and I always wept inconsolably when it was time to come home.

All of this combined to take me to Selwyn College, Cambridge University to study languages (French and Spanish). I had always hoped to go to one of the cool, fun Northern Universities with an amazing social scene but when I got the Cambridge offer, I felt it would be a mistake to decline.

It was a good decision in so many ways; it was certainly not a nightlife hotbed but I made some friends for life there and there have been times in my life when the fact that I had studied there meant people who had decided upon meeting me that I was probably not intelligent needed to think again (I know I am not the only woman who has faced this bias). But most importantly, Cambridge was where I met my (now ex) husband and my son Joe was made and born, and for this reason alone going there was the best decision I ever made.

He was born just after my second-year exams and I had to sit them in a special room because I couldn't fit into the exam hall desk with my baby bump! People tell me they are impressed that I still managed to finish my degree but, frankly, I think it's much easier to handle being a student with a young child than it is to do a full-time job that requires you to be in the office at dawn and be full-on all day, no matter how many times you were up in the night – which is what most of the women I know have needed to do. That's what's really heroic.

As soon as I graduated, I started my career at Procter & Gamble (P&G) in the Marketing Department in the suburbs of Surrey. No sabbatical for me, I had big debts to pay (as you can imagine, a student grant doesn't quite cover Cambridge Day Nursery costs) but I was also very keen to start working. The idea of working on famous brands and their marketing plans was extremely exciting to me and I never lost this thrill. I have worked on global leading brands like Pantene, Head & Shoulders, Olay, Max Factor, Always and Tampax and I loved and still love every single one of them. They are incredible brands and products and it was a privilege to contribute to making them even stronger. To this day there is nothing I love more than the challenge of building or fixing a brand.

My son Joe was a year old when I started at P&G so I needed to find a way to fit my work into a 9-6 day (his nursery hours). I'm actually really glad of that because it meant that, from day one, I had to work this way; most people there were working 12 plus hour days (because they could) and then had to adjust later if or when they became parents, which was tougher for them I think.

I admit that I was concerned I wouldn't be able to compete with my peers who were working such long hours, but I could and it didn't hold me back from being promoted quickly to Brand Manager, Marketing Director and ultimately Senior Vice President. I actually believe that being a mum from the start and having a hard 'nursery closing' deadline every day forced me to be focused on delivering the big priorities. I think we are all guilty of being less efficient when we have more time available.

After 12 years, I was moved to Geneva to get global brand and business experience. I was not thrilled by the prospect but it turned out to be one of the best things I ever did. It was amazing to experience the power of the diversity in those teams, with people from every country, origin and culture. I learnt so much about business, about people, about the world. And this was where I also learnt about the gender equality issue and was ultimately inspired to write a book about it.

I had of course been aware of gender diversity issues before, but I had personally never been on the wrong end of them. I had never felt in any way held back as a woman and, to be honest, I didn't understand why people made an issue of it. I am rather ashamed to admit that I used to be one of those women who was rather dismissive of women who complained about gender inequality. And then I finally saw it, even though it was almost invisible – and I became absolutely fascinated by it.

I could see it was happening and I could see the impact it was having on women, but I wanted to understand the reasons why. So, I watched, listened, devoured as many books and articles as I could – and this made me realise the extent of it, that women everywhere were facing and struggling with these dynamics, that men were winning at work and women were usually, ultimately, losing.

Despite the stacks of research and unequivocal data that shows that gender equality leads to stronger teams, stronger businesses and stronger societies, wherever we look (business, sport, politics, healthcare, wherever) we see that the people in the leadership positions are 90% men. I was asking myself why, if women have equal leadership ability, are they so under-represented at the top levels in business and society? Why are we still living in a man's world, and why do we accept it?

And so, I made a promise to myself, that when I left my job, I would write a book about this. It's time for us to stop being positive, patient and polite about gender inequality. We need to stop accepting it and start acting with a sense of urgency now to make some real progress. I hope my book (*Why Men Win at Work*, just published) can contribute to that.

This is very much the start of a new chapter in my story then, living in my beloved France and with the freedom to work for myself, the way I choose and on what is important to me. I loved my job but now I hope that I will be able to help companies, organisations and individuals to drive gender equality and diversity with my work as a speaker, consultant and coach. I love it every time I see the 'penny drop moment' happen and it fills me with huge optimism that we can change things and we can, together, make inequality history.

JANNETTE BARRETT

Founder
JAN CAN CARE

Jancancare1@gmail.com

CHAPTER 8

The Belief Seed

What makes us do what we do? What stirs our passions and steers us to drive to the top of our game? 'The Belief Seed'. We use the word 'faith' and we use the phrase 'gut instincts' for this sometimes but I like to use, 'the belief seed' to describe the deep feeling we have over certain things. Why do I use that phrase? Well many seeds are blown in the air, many are deliberately planted and some are digested before being either regurgitated or defecated out, but all or at least most grow even the ones we don't want grown, weeds. That's what business can be like. It can grow well but sometimes every now and then you have to do some tactile weeding.

Where did your seed of belief come from? Was it planted in you by your own expectations or was it a seed planted in you by someone else? An idea passed and passed on the winds of voice? These are important questions, because self-belief is the key to success, well that's what I was told. If I didn't plant the seed of success within myself and continued to rely on others to build my self-esteem, I may never grow that seed to full bloom because I had no belief, no faith, no gut instinct in myself for it to bloom. I'm still sitting on the fence with those questions, because my self-belief was rock bottom when I started my business. It took a number of people telling me I could achieve anything I put my mind too, they could see what I couldn't. Has that happened with you?

I started my business 'Jan Can Care' in 2004, purely due to being totally fed up with everything being against the clock. Prior to starting out on my own, I was working two jobs. One was in the blood bank, where I shared the task of taking the initial pipette blood samples of donors to check their haemoglobin levels and the other was at Selly Oak hospital first on the nursing care side of things, then a few years in the radiography department trying to find the satisfaction of making a real difference to people's lives, something was always missing. In hindsight I think it was because I wasn't complete. Both of those jobs were based in Birmingham but I had a spell in London too doing nursing, under very different circumstances.

Why I actually choose the nursing care profession may come as a bit of a shock to you, then again; it may make perfect sense. I can only put it down to the fact I was a young carer. Quite frankly, I should have run in the complete opposite direction, due to the fact that the majority of that period in my life, being so blooming awful. Don't take my words wrongly, I love my sister to bits and in many ways, she's been the making of me. Maybe in hindsight I'm a complete coward and chose nursing care because I didn't want to jump out of that 'unusual' comfort zone, I grew so accustomed to. Truth be known, I still don't one hundred percent know why I choose nursing! Except that I happen to be really good at it.

My schooling was riddled with uncertainties whilst looking out for my sister's wellbeing, being a young carer at school was a difficult task. I was always torn and tormented by guilt over the things I felt. I didn't for a minute enjoy being taken out of class to sit and calm her when she felt anxious, oh no I didn't think that was fair on me at all. It wasn't her fault, of course, that she has autism.

Autism has a very wide spectrum of symptoms and some are not easily noticed. Needless to say, due to these absences from class I had to work really hard to catch up on class and homework. I didn't even realise at the time why I found working on things by myself so difficult but there was certainly a very valid reason indeed. I was dyslexic. All this resulted in me having quite a few challenges when trying to make the business operative.

I was actually assessed for dyslexia whilst training to become a psychiatric nurse in London. My practical skills were exemplary but my coursework needed plenty of guidance, all of which I obtained and am forever grateful for. I'm a proud dyslexic now mind you, and I should be. My business has been running now for sixteen years with most clients coming from word of mouth reference. My name now proceeds me. Never In a million years would I ever have envisaged saying that or anyone endorsing me for who I am, personally, let alone my variety of skills.

I'll have you know that it's only due to the lockdown crisis we have been faced with that I've learned to use the zoom app, but I still, for the life of me, cannot copy and paste and I just cringe and coil when it comes to invoices, or paying monies into another person's account and likewise. Challenges oh yes, I certainly have a few but my drive and passion push me to continue regardless.

We never stop learning, do we? Being a dyslexic, can make that learning process feel really powerful or it can make you feel powerless. The difference between 'getting it' and struggling to 'get it' is as wide for me as an ocean divide. When I get it, my delight is of an extremely high frequency, you cannot take me off the ceiling for days. When I struggle, even the soles of my feet are higher than my head yet I keep going.

Dyslexia is a two-edged sword to me, it helps me cut my way through the harshest things to learn, with a sharp witty tongue, but that same sharp tongue will also critique me into my own shell again in a nanosecond. It's a balance I have to keep a mindful eye on.

I am fortunate however to have the ability to perform, I can perform in front of anyone in any space at any given time, even if spontaneously asked to do so. This inspires me to face things head on and always fills me with confidence. The ability to perform at the drop of a hat didn't come lightly though, it came from a necessity to be seen and heard. As a child I didn't feel I was being seen or heard and that drifted into my adult years. Ironically, now I love to perform and absorb the energies of my audience. Talk about flipping the coin eh!

With my nursing care skills accompanied with my performance skills, I believe I have a unique combination that has enhanced my personality to keep growing and glowing. Empathy is a gifted skill, it helps me to really listen, knowledge of care helps me to see what others may not see. Both empathy and care also assist me to engage with others openly and that builds trust. Trust can build successes and successes can build confidence.

The advice I often give to people is to never try to be who they are not. I quote "be you, stay true and always follow through in all you do". Why is that so important? It's important because it's honest. Nobody can stay fake for too long or enjoy being so, believe me, I wore a masked personality for decades; it's exhausting and you end up not recognising who the hell you are.

Stick with the true you, after all you are unique, so you are giving people the chance to learn, engage and work with an original 'Jane or John Doe'.

When they try to emulate you, let them be your clone copy, until they get their vision to flourish. Tell them also to be true to themselves. I think that's the best advice to give to anyone because it's the only advice that can build 'the belief seed'.

JOANNE OUTRAM

Founder
FINANCIAL FITNESS CLUB

Jooutram.com
jo@financialfitnessclub.co.uk

CHAPTER 9

It's About More Than Money

I was stood there, aged 42, on my parent's doorstep needing somewhere to live. I had gone from £1million net worth to being over £100k in the negative, and full of shame. For a finance professional, this shame weighed far heavier than the debt.

The road to arriving at this position although long, was not always arduous as there had been plenty interludes of the high life. There had been warning signs though. If you don't know that you need glasses and are constantly looking down, you can even miss enormous 'danger ahead' signs! Even if they are fifty feet high with neon flashing lights.

Let's take a few steps back and look at how I got there. Like many people, I fell into my career. I always loved numbers, and accountancy seemed like an excellent subject to study at University. After graduating I landed a job with one of the top accountancy firms. Out of the 13 of us who started the gruelling three years of training in my office, I was one of only four who made it to the other side. I felt an overwhelming sense of commitment to this choice in career.

Exciting times lay ahead, except for the fact that I had nearly a year off work due to illness. This was burnout number one. Although burnout wasn't a term used back then.

After six months of struggling back at work, I felt ready to look for another job. I found one with an accounting practice, which was local to my family, allowing me to sell up and move back to my hometown.

Fast forward two and a half years, and shortly after my 29th birthday, I was made partner. At this point, I was the youngest female partner in a firm of Chartered Accountants, at a time when there were not even many women in partnership roles.

Just before my 30th birthday, I had left the partnership and was on my own. Not out of any desire to branch out but forced to find a way out. It was my time to step into the solopreneur role, and like most who start on this journey, I had plenty of saleable skills but no business acumen.

Within my first year, I had purchased a stunning Georgian office building and acquired an accountancy practice to absorb into mine. Things were going great, and my business was starting to expand. With the encouragement of my co-owner of the office, I had undertaken my professional exams to become an Independent Financial Advisor. I was excited and ready to explore new ideas. Having discovered a company that coached accountancy firms on how to grow their business and how to develop business coaching services, I took my entire staff to their annual conference.

During one session at the conference, a female solo-preneur accountant (a rare breed in those days) was on stage talking about the fantastic things she had done to grow her practice. I declared to my team that I would be on the stage next year. Without knowing it, I was about to use the Law of Attraction. I had set my intention, and I believed, without doubt, that it was possible.

I took every opportunity to learn and develop my business and there I was at the next annual conference on stage talking about all the wonderful ways in which my firm had developed. I was asked to speak at their next event, and the one after that. In fact, after three years of speaking at all their conferences, I did suggest that people might be fed up with hearing from me!

It opened many new doors. At one event I was talking to a director of an outsourcing company in India. He offered me a minority share in the company and a directorship. I grasped the opportunity and let's say that having travelled to India, it's an experience. The contrast between the poor and the wealthy is staggering and has to be seen to be believed.

Back home in the UK, with my growing business, the time was right to give something back to the community. Soon after, I saw an advert in the local newspaper, which I seldom read, for a governor at the local college, who was preferably female and with experience of finance. As the only applicant and fitting all their criteria I was hired.

One month in and things started to get interesting when the new CEO announced that he wanted to expand the scope of the college and build a new campus. A year later and after overcoming some internal politics, I was the youngest chairman of a UK college.

The next few years were exhausting, with relentless meetings with bank managers, funding council representatives, local officials, top civil servants from London, MPs from the surrounding boroughs and not to mention four different Education Ministers who each needed to be briefed on the most substantial capital build under their remit.

At this time, of being a director in a company in India, which was now going through a buy-out; of being the Chairman of a board on an institution with circa £30 million in revenue, over 1,500 members of staff and undertaking a £70 million capital project; running my accountancy practice which now had 15 team members over two offices and outsourced staff based in India, I somehow believed that I could take something else on. Why as women do we do this?

I was offered the chance to bring an Australian/US training company over to the UK. Of course, I quickly said "yes!" It was an exciting time that allowed me to deliver training in places such as Sydney and Las Vegas.

On stage in Las Vegas, ten minutes into giving a keynote speech to a packed room of accountants, and I have an 'aha' moment. One of those moments that's a true turning point. The realisation that I didn't want a career where I stood in front of 500 people and talked. Not the best timing but it certainly grabbed my attention.

Now at a crossroads in my career I did have the common sense to hire a coach. Better late than never! The coach I chose was ex-special forces and a recently retired Major from the British Army. Unfortunately, his help arrived too late, and the inevitable burn out soon followed.

This time was different, burnout as a business owner often prevents you from hitting the pause button, as you have no choice but to carry on. I was after all responsible for the mortgages of a dozen families.

Over the next 18 months, the manager at my accountancy practice left and set out to destroy my business. There's a saying about a woman scorned, well it's equally true of men. A business partner in the coaching business, also proved to be a costly mistake as he was an emotional bully. Under his influence I sold the accountancy practice. This would have been a fantastic move, if I had been able to keep all the sale proceeds, to pay off debts etc.

This was around the time of the property crash, so add into the mix the anxiety over money and a house I needed to vacate as I couldn't afford it any longer, I fell further into depression. I'm sure some people were saying, "how the mighty have fallen", and it certainly was how I felt.

This is where this story began, age 42, on my parent's doorstep.

When the time was right to start pulling myself together, I found a temp job and rediscovered that I had skills. This led me to a role where I ultimately became the finance director. I spent five years working for this company. I went from having debts to having savings, and the company went from low multi 6-figures to multi 7-figures in income. More importantly I discovered, that my near divorce from money combined with all my skills acquired over the years in business meant I was uniquely placed to help other women in business get a handle on how they deal with money. This was a good and most welcome 'aha' moment.

That's where the Money Mindset work comes into play. Money is such an emotional subject and how we think about it is so important. However, it's not a get rich quick scheme. It took me over 3 years to clear my debts and 7 years before I acquired a share in property, with no mortgage, and bought my BMW for cash.

I believe that everything happens for a reason though, and we are given specific paths and challenges to make us into the person we are today. This is my purpose in life and my new role – to help women in business improve their relationship with money so that they can avoid their version of financial ruin and instead achieve a life of abundance.

<u>JO HALEY</u>

THE POSITIVE IMAGE COACH MFIPI

Thepositiveimagecoach.co.uk
jo@thepositiveimagecoach.co.uk

CHAPTER 10

Igniting Your Identity

L oved working at the hotel. Every day was always different but this was the day when my life was going to change...

As I walked through the bar area to get to the staff room, I stopped and chatted to the couple having their morning coffee, cleared some plates from the gentlemen having their meeting and walked into the servery to say hello to the rest of the team. It was definitely another busy day. We had a conference being held in the Buckmaster Suite, the bistro was fully booked at lunch and the main restaurant was getting busier by the second too. For the week, I personally had been looking after the men in the conference room, they were from a local car dealer in town. While they broke for lunch on their last day, I went in to clear and tidy the room and then I saw it - I had no idea which man had done this but knew that I would find out.

Jen, my best friend at college and I had not been back long from travelling the world together. We spent an incredible 8 months back packing our way around different countries, seeing some amazing sites, doing some crazy activities and meeting incredible people. We had an absolute ball.

Being with and meeting new people is something I have always loved doing. I suppose being brought up in the hotel industry threw me into that but also, I am a lover of life. Having a very happy disposition means that I find talking to strangers fairly easy. I love being nosey, to discover what they love doing, where they live and what they do so I knew how lucky I was to have a job back at the hotel after this trip.

Back in the conference room I was clearing up the coffee cups, replacing the water bottle, glasses and straightening up the writing pads, blotters and pens. That was when I saw it – one of these men had drawn my necklace, the one I wore every day on their writing pad with the word 'drink?' underneath it. I had no idea which gentleman had done that but I had a choice of 12!

Walking back to the restaurant my heart was all a flutter and I could feel his eyes looking at me. We ended up going for a drink the next day and before I knew it our relationship had blossomed and we were living together. It was hard at first as we had a lot of challenges and obstacles to overcome but eventually, we moved into his marital home and at the age of 21, I became a Mummy to his two children, four-year-old Annie and 2-year-old Tom (names changed). Times were tough, good mixed with the bad, but we just got on with life as you do.

It all changed one night, just like that and out of nowhere, I can still remember the argument now, in the bedroom and then bang, he hit me in the face and stormed off down stairs. I could see Annie standing in the doorway asking if I was ok, she couldn't see me like this, not after what her daddy had done to me. Of course, he apologised and said it would never happen again.

Time went by, so did the beatings, the hurt and the anger. What had I ever done apart from be there for him and his children? My parents sold the hotel, moved away to a new town and I was still living in this turmoil of a relationship knowing that I wanted out but just didn't know how. It wasn't just physical but mentally and emotionally abusive too.

Beauty had always been a real interest to me and so I found a Cosmetology course where my parents lived and so started slowly to get away. I spent the weeks with my parents, they never knew about my situation, then back to his on the weekend, knowing that when the course finished after a year, I would never go back. That was my plan. During the course, I got a job as a Beauty Consultant working in a large department store and I was loving it. New friends, new plans and was feeling free, but then in a blink of an eye, it all changed again.

I had just finished my client's makeup and as I looked up, there he was, smiling and grinning from ear to ear delighted he had found me. Little did I know he had sorted the kids who had gone back to live with their mother. He had found a job in the town where I lived and sorted us a house, we were going to be together again. Maybe it will be ok this time, he was in a better job and seemed a lot happier and so once again, I moved back in.

The beatings didn't stop, the abuse, the anger, the curfews, they all continued whilst I was a Beauty Consultant. Covering up my black eyes at work and bruising on my arms was hard but I had my own line of customers who I would give makeup lessons too and facials. I became the Manageress of our own Beauty Lounge and still, no one knew. No one knew what I was going through. The Beauty Consultant behind the counter helping others to feel worthy and special.

Helping others to look after themselves, to value themselves, giving them a boost of self-esteem and a heap of confidence to be the woman they truly are. Every time I looked in the mirror, I had to believe that I was that woman too.

Five years passed. That's how long it took for me to leave. The night I left was horrendous, the beatings and kicking I had but I did it, I found the strength to really do it, to leave for good and never go back.

I trained as an Image Coach 14 years ago not because I am a follower of fashion or an 'on-trend' kind of gal but because I realised that there is far more to beauty then being aesthetically pleasing. It is about you as a whole person. How you look and feel about yourself are so important and I firmly believe that as ladies, we absolutely do not value ourselves enough. As women we go through so many transitions in our lives but along the way we lose who we are, our identity, our self-esteem, confidence and self-worth. Our wardrobes are often bursting at the seams with clothes from different stages of our lives but knowing who you are is key to being beautiful.

Four years ago, I went and did some more training and took my Masters in Image. This means that I am accredited by City & Guilds and one of only 20 people in the world with this qualification and I am a member of the Federation of Image Professionals. This was so hard for me to do as I am not about styling or fashion. I had to really learn and understand so much more about image and how getting dressed is really about creating optical illusions and works of art – but it is so worth it.

In my role as The Positive Image Coach, I see women who are deflated. It is my job (and passion) to show them how great they truly are and how their body is beautiful just by being uniquely their own. I educate them on how to dress so that they can shine, feel empowered and reclaim their identity. My aim is to help women to be the best version of themselves, all day, every day so that when they walk out of their front door, they can be proud of who they are, who they have become and walk that stage in style.

My story came out for the very first time this year, back in February. The crazy thing was, the night before it was launched, I heard a domestic fight go on in the block of flats I live in. I couldn't lay there in bed and do nothing, so ran downstairs, outside to find this girl, wearing just a sweatshirt and underwear, with blood on her hands and face – I looked into her eyes and at that moment, it was just like looking in the mirror all those years ago. I have never been confronted with it before or since but one thing is for sure, it has changed my life on so many levels. Yes, I have a very happy outlook on life. Yes, I am a very positive person but I know that I am scarred from those years in many ways and am still working on myself every day.

JO VAN OSCH

Business Psychologist & Executive Coach
INSPIRED AT WORK LTD

inspiredatwork.co.uk
jo@inspiredatwork.co.uk

CHAPTER 11

A Quest For Purpose

Last year, I started a new chapter in my business journey with a company founded on purpose and doing business for good – Inspired at work Ltd. The ultimate mission of the company is to solve what in my view is a big problem in our workplaces – unhappiness, unfulfilled potential, compromised mental health and burnout. Doing business for good means that the company seeks to support and contribute to the United Nations sustainable goal for decent work for all. Helping companies to create more inspired, psychologically safe and sustainable workplaces where people can thrive. Where leaders can lead with compassion, courage and humility, and where teams work together productively to create and innovate.

It is my quest for living and working on purpose that has brought me here, and I am happy to share my story with you. Many times, along my journey, I wondered whether I was ever going to find my elusive purpose, and you may be experiencing something similar. My quest for purpose was in no way straight forward, there were mountains to climb and oceans to cross. Sometimes, I got lost, and it took me a while to get back on track. On my journey, I found pieces of the purpose puzzle. Some pieces did fit in straight away, others didn't seem to fit at all. At least not at first sight. Some pieces didn't fit until, in some cases many years later, they just fell into place.

I was born in The Netherlands, my mum was a stay-at-home mum, my dad was a brilliant social worker with some very challenging clients. By the time I went to primary school, I was all too aware of the dangers of people who had - let's say not such good intentions. To keep me safe, I had to be brought to school where I was then bullied because of that. At home, the tension was high. Every night, my mom and I waited until my dad came home safe. The threats, the calls to the police, and the memories of drawing the curtains with the lights off and staying quiet are still vivid. When we finally moved city and I went to a different school, the bullying stopped, and the tension at home lessened. When my dad's boss asked me whether I wanted to become a social worker, just like my dad when I grew up, I cried. I was so aware of how fragile life can be, and I was certainly not planning on following a career that involved helping people. To me, at seven years old, that spelt danger.

I really didn't like school, I was very bored, tried to be invisible and did the absolute minimum to pass. I didn't feel like I belonged. After secondary school, things changed. I started to like studying. I studied tourism at first – just because it was only one-year fast-tracked learning – and then went on the university to become a translator. I only stayed for a year. I loved languages and different cultures, but translating wasn't doing it for me.

My first business I started at the age of 21, straight out of college because I couldn't find any work. Armed with my language skills - writing, editing, translating - I became what you would now call a VA.

How hard could it be to figure it out?

It turned out to be a very steep learning curve, but learning I did. I found my passion for continuous learning in that part of the quest. And still today, I am a learning addict – professional skills, personal development, spiritual development you name it. I learnt everything I possibly could from marketing, PR, sales, bookkeeping, HR to computer skills. And, I discovered psychology pulling on my heartstrings, including the wonderful world of neuro-linguistic programming (NLP) which satisfied my love for languages. The market was extremely competitive, and eventually, I took a job alongside the business to pay the bills. Burning the candle at both ends sound familiar?

I found a job as an Executive Assistant which I really enjoyed. My boss was great, and I had some excellent opportunities to develop myself professionally. When I was made redundant, I was responsible for the HR in the branch and successfully recruited 150 staff as the only person out of all branches without a degree in hr. The head of HR came to see me wanting to know how I achieved such a high retention rate. I couldn't answer that question back then, I just talked with people, finding out whether they were a good match. That's all. Despite loving the job and achieving great success, it was also the time when I experienced my first burnout. On reflection, caring too much and taking on too much responsibility came at a high cost. The redundancy came as a blessing. I also knew what I wanted to do next – training. With the learning I took from my first business venture, I started out in business again and quickly turned it into success this time around. Being able to plan my own time also helped me to recover from the burnout while doing work that I loved. Training didn't feel like work at all to me.

I also tried to study psychology at university during this time, but I couldn't get through the statistics courses. Back then, it was all manual calculations, definitely not my favourite thing. Something more practical was what I wanted, and I found a counselling course. I absolutely loved it! The apple didn't fall far from the tree, after all. At the end of my second year, I came to the realisation that counselling was what I was doing at home, every single day. I left my husband over that summer holiday and moved to Spain for a while. At that time, we were also running a recruitment and training business together, which made things a bit complicated. I decided to close the business to cut the ties completely. It felt like the best decision I could make, not with my head, but from my heart and gut instinct.

Back to a 'proper job' I went, and I completed the last two years of my counselling course. This time I became a customer service and training manager with a team of

36. There was zero trust when I started, so I had my job cut out. I worked long hours, winning the trust of the team members, coached them individually and as a team to help them perform at their best. Again, I was like a fish in water. But as before, I reverted back to burning the candle at both ends and burnout struck once again. I decided it was time for a massive change – get out of corporate and move to the UK.

Soon after I arrived in the UK, I found a job working in my favourite spiritual shop. I had been on a path of spiritual development since my teens, so this offered me a great opportunity to do something completely different. I took a lot of spiritual and personal development learning from that time, and I also started to accumulate certifications in a range of therapeutic modalities. I found a different job, this time in the council's housing department. My dad passed away in 2010, the week after I talked to him about going back to university to complete a psychology degree. That conversation was what kept me going in difficult times. I just couldn't give up.

In 2011, while still working in my housing officer job, I took the leap to start my own counselling and hypnotherapy practice. A few years later, I added coaching to the mix. In developing my practice, I worked with some business mentors and coaches over the years. It's something that I didn't have when I first started. Having a good business coach is absolutely priceless. I had some excellent guidance, but also some awful advice that nearly cost me my passion for my work. What I learnt was to follow my heart and gut feeling. I began to specialise in working with workplace-related issues, stress, anxiety and burnout because I noticed that that was what I enjoyed most.

My business focus pivoted when I was completing my master's degree in occupational psychology. I could see that the issues that I had been working with needed to be addressed more systemically. The idea for Inspired at work Ltd was born. I also learned about social enterprise, and that resonated very much for me - combining business and social impact. The missing piece – an inspired business with a mission to do good.

My story is still unfolding. I'm still learning to be visible. My quest continues with a new focus, it is no longer a quest for purpose, but one on purpose. At 49, I'm starting a doctorate in organisational psychology. My learning never ends. My desire to make a difference is greater than ever.

KATY DYZEWSKA

Coach | Trainer | Speaker
KATY D BUSINESS COACH

edutainer@katydyzewska.com
KatyDBusinessCoaching.com

CHAPTER 12

A Bubble Misfit Who Tried To Fit

My name is Katy and I am an economist.

Sounds like the start of an AA meeting, but it isn't. It's a story of a woman who felt lost for a long time in her life. Who wanted to please others more than to listen to herself? Who tried to fit in, but was too tall, too loud and too lively for most people?

THE BEGINNING

When I was a little girl, my granddad asked me: "Why aren't you like other girls?" So, I cried.

A 'friend' in primary school said: "Why are you so fast?" So, I tried to slow down, felt frustrated and cried.

Other girls said: "You are crazy!" So, I stopped talking, and I cried.

I played with boys. They accepted me and were OK with me on the football field as a goalkeeper. I was finally a good fit (plus I was an excellent goalkeeper and never let the ball pass). However, it was a boys' group. I was a girl. I was still in the wrong group. I was judged; I shouldn't be catching the ball I should be sitting with the girls and talking about lip gloss. So, I stopped and I cried.

No matter where I went, I had to be the 'right' fit. Like a chameleon, I was changing myself to adapt to the world of others, to fit in and be one of them. However, when I could be, I was myself. A girl full of sound, colours and positive attitude; with the ability to speak in front of others (no matter how big the audience) and to organise things brilliantly. That is me. No fear. No crying. No need to fit in. Just me. But as a kid, I wanted to be like others and be have their approval.

BURNOUT

Let me get back to the economist part of me. I have a brother, who was always the best in my eyes. He is about eight years older than me, and he was and will always be the best brother.

He was also the best in the eyes of my granddad.

When I was a kid, I wanted my grandad's approval. I wanted to be the best in his eyes. I wanted him to notice and approve of me.

When I was a child, I couldn't be the best, because I was a girl and always too little to take anywhere. But then when it came to choosing my university degree, I could get his approval. I thought economics is the right choice: it will make him happy.

He always said there are only two jobs that matter: undertaker and economist. Being an undertaker wasn't appealing to me, so an economist it was.

Also, my brother studied it and I love maths.

The only problem: I also had a dream. I wanted to be an actress. Despite all the negative things I had heard about that profession like:

- there is no money in it,
- you have to be super talented,
- you have to be beautiful to make it,
- you are too fragile to make it, and
- you need to know someone on the inside.

So, even though my family was important, I decided to give acting a try.

I enrolled.

I went through the first levels, but in the end, I flinched: would they approve of me being me?

At the final entry exam, I blew it.

Instead of acting school, I went to a private economic school. I was good at it. I found a job at the fourth year of university, and shortly after graduation, I went to work and live in Luxembourg, where I still am.

When I look back to those times, I was numb.

I met great people and enjoyed my time being a student. I studied abroad for a while, travelled and finally moved to a country that speaks all languages. A fantastic life isn't it? However, slowly I was falling into a burnout mode. Job after job I was not feeling fulfilled.

The finance world expected me to be a together; a quiet introvert and do my job as it is, with no need for the process be improved. Nobody believed (and still do not) that a bubbly extrovert can be an economist or to be precise be a digit focused accountant. Again, I was too different when I was me.

Another job with more responsibility came up. I thought, I am going to be amazing, but why should I even try? Why should I be myself? I'd better hide and be like they want me to be. I'd better just fit in. I was falling into misery and sadness. Instead of beautiful dresses and suits, I wore black sweat pants to the office. Nobody noticed. I stopped wearing makeup. Nobody even saw that.

I am not a woman who gives up. I didn't want to let myself fall into depression. Instead of doctors and pills, I looked for self-development books. I learned about entrepreneurship and myself. I got back to the source and let myself dream again. I woke up the girl, who is loud, happy, confident, well organised and has the talent to speak without fear.

SPEAK, LEAD, BUILD YOUR BRAND

The main turning point in my career was joining the Masters in Business Administration studies. I wanted to learn more about business and see what else I could do with my knowledge.

I quickly confirmed my feeling:

A prosperous company means people. How they feel, how they think, how they act. I learnt a lot from my fellow students. I also realised that my life's mission is to support people in achieving their goals and making their dreams come true. People I studied with saw the bubbly girl who can change the world and make things happen. Most of them told me that I was not an accounting type. "You were not created to sit behind a desk," said a girl, I met on the first day.

They saw in me someone who is good with people, someone who has a talent to speak, someone who can help others flourish.

I kept discovering myself, and I realised that the best way to use my passion for business and people is via developing coaching and training programs.

I am a natural speaker. I inspire and teach via my YouTube Channel and via live and online events. My first work as an entrepreneur was to help other women find their voice and the way to be brave, to stand in front of an audience and speak. I am assisting small businesses run by women to find their voice. I help them organise their speeches, to make them enjoyable from start to finish.

I am a leader, and my main interest is to create confident CEOs. I am not talking only about company CEOs, but most of all CEOs of life. Women who can take their life in their hands and lead it to make their dreams come true.

I am a brand and business strategist. I am a holder of a Master's Degree in Economics and a Master's in Business Administration. I am a certified Business Trainer and Coach. Connecting all my talents, I help change a shy brand into a shiny one.

I DON'T TRY TO FIT IN

I am no longer the girl who tried to fit. Why should I fit in? I am an amazing woman, and so are you!

It took me a while to transform my life, but I have the confidence that I can not only change my future but also help you transform yours. The main challenge I thought I faced was the environment that never seemed to believe in me. In reality, I did not believe in myself. I believed in all blocks that other people had. However, those were never my beliefs, and those were never my limitations. Now I can see that, and I can help others build their confident presence. I know that with each step my clients make they are becoming the CEO of their own life.

If you read this, it means you are looking to change, and that you are looking to be inspired. I can only hope that with my story, you will be able to make your next step to change without fear. That you will be able to seek help and change the way you think, to start to believe in yourself. To believe that you have the strength to live your dream.

THE FUTURE

The future ahead is inspiring. No matter what the day will bring, I will keep going. I have ideas for three books, and I will find time to write them. I am building my message for the world step by step, and I hope to talk to you one day. One day, I wish to say I helped a million women change their lives to live in abundance, happiness and confidence. An actual club of CEOs of life.

KIMBERLY HAMBRICK

CEO | President
KIMBERLY HAMBRICK CONSULTING LLC

Kimberlyhambrick.com
hambrick.kimberlya@gmail.com

CHAPTER 13

My Life Reset

In my early 50s I resigned from my corporate position of almost 30 years—without a safety-net or a plan. Though not planned, it was the right decision. Many thought I was having a mid-life crisis, but for me, it was a mid-life awakening. I was finally awakened to my own value and worth.

For as long as I can remember, I had self-limiting beliefs. I struggled for years with what followed "I AM ...". Two simple words, yet when I used them, I heard myself say "I AM not worthy." "I AM not good enough." "I AM not loved."

From the outside looking in, I appeared happy and successful. From the inside, I battled my own BS, belief system or the bullshit swirl of negative thoughts and excuses.

I desperately wanted others to tell me I mattered. I never truly looked at my unique worthiness. I was well into my 40s when I realised that I had been marginalising myself by failing to claim my own worthiness.

A few people in my life who knew I suffered from this, took advantage. Several colleagues kept "Kimmyisms" on their phones, things that I said incorrectly. I have never once claimed to be perfect and at times I mangle words.

But as someone who suffered from limiting self-beliefs, to be reminded of my mistakes time and time again and laughed at by people that I respected, only added to my BS swirl. Another colleague started every conversation with "Do you know what your problem is?" Within seconds I was buying into "my problem" hook, line, and sinker.

Life Reset

It wasn't until my 50s that I finally busted through my own BS and reset my life. The gut-kicks of my life, the ones that took my breath away and made me pause, were the catalysts I needed to finally see my own value and worth. The last one came about when a "friend and a colleague" that I trusted completely shared a personal situation about my youngest son with the CEO of the company. I was stunned that he would do this and I said, "It's not your story to share; those that needed to know knew about it."

My calling him out on this pushed him to develop and share a 30 plus page document about my behaviour. The content was created by his 10 plus years of recording me. Almost from the first day we started working together.

The recordings included audio and video recordings and pages and pages of journal notes—all done without my knowledge or consent. My "friend" was building a catalogue of tidbits to weave into a story, if and when needed. Once I got over the initial feelings of shock and betrayal, I realized that no one else thought his actions were extreme, or even illegal. I heard myself say "I resign". I knew that I had to remove myself from this situation and the toxic environment and find a different path forward. I knew that to do this successfully, I had to address my limiting self-beliefs. When you hit the bottom, you either stay there or pull yourself up. I knew that I could not do this alone.

Following my resignation, I reached out and worked with several mentors of the John Maxwell team. I joined the team about three months prior to my resignation. My main reason for joining was to become a better leader and effectively impact the lives of others. I had NO idea that the life that would be impacted the most was my own. My turning point came with the guidance of two mentors. In talking with one and explaining my situation, he said "You have to own the truth of this situation that is yours to own and let the rest go".

WOW! This was completely foreign to me. I had to lean into this and look at the situation and myself in the mirror. I realised my limiting self-beliefs were attracting the wrong people into my circle. People who would intentionally try to destroy me personally, professionally, financially, and emotionally.

As a highly-educated and successful woman, this was difficult to accept. But my constant need for validation made me an easy target for others, and in all honesty, had me displaying actions, at times, that were not always of high standards.

In terms of my "friend" who stalked me, I won't accept the responsibility for his extreme actions. That had absolutely nothing to do with me and everything to do with him. He obviously had some issues that drove him to such bizarre behaviour. I have blessed and released this person. This simple yet profound act has empowered me beyond measure.

Another mentor showed me how to become the first believer in myself by telling me to "borrow the belief I have in you, until your belief matches mine". Every time I think about his words to me, I cry. I have never had anyone speak into me like that, let alone someone that I didn't really know, in that he said this to me on my first call with him. His belief prompted me to do exactly as he said, believe in me. I borrowed his belief and clung to it as I moved forward because, I AM worth it.

I began to pay close attention to the voices I allowed to speak into my life. I also did the work to make my voice the loudest and the one I listened to the most. For the first time in my life, in my early 50s, I focused intently on my growth.

I started to take notice of the number of times a day, sub-consciously or not, that I followed "I AM" with a negative or self-limiting word. What an eye-opener! I couldn't believe how effortlessly I said things about myself that I would never say about anyone else. And I worked to change that internal dialogue. Today, my "I AM" is followed by "beautiful," "competent," and "loved." This simple yet profound mindset shift has opened my eyes to my worthiness. I no longer seek outside validation. "I AM enough!"

In the past, another person's view of me had the potential to send me into a spiral of negative thoughts. I doubted myself so much that someone else's view became my view of me. Then I added that negative thought into my limiting self-belief suitcase until it became a three-piece set of luggage that weighed me down and kept me stuck.

Those moments still creep in, but they do not have the same effect on me as they had in the past. When a negative thought bubbles up, I quickly realise it as negative and then I take a pause and ask myself "Is there truth in this thought or not?"

If the answer is no, I quickly dismiss and move forward. If the answer is yes, I then determine what I can control and change versus what I can't control. This simple yet profound step of focusing on what I can control and change has improved the quality of my life greatly.

For example, if someone shares a negative opinion about me and I see a kernel of truth in it, I focus on what I can control. Spending energy on trying to change someone's opinion of me is useless energy. I get to decide to change my behaviour if it's important to me to change. This is where my power resides.

I accepted responsibility for my actions, exited several toxic relationships, and focused intentionally on moving myself forward. I was in unchartered waters—standing up for myself for the first time in my life and truly believing in myself. But it felt right. A first step was to decide what I wanted to do with my life. What makes me sing? What makes me come alive? What makes me dream? Focusing on these questions allowed me the space to find my passion. As the direction became clear, my fears of the unknown eased and my excitement built. I saw a path forward that allowed me to fully embrace my gifts and start my own consulting company.

The past few years have been the most personally and professionally satisfying for me. I was successful in my past. My accomplishments were great. But now, my accomplishments are greater and I am striving for extraordinary.

It is never too late for us to reset our lives and to fully live into our gifts. We owe it to ourselves to be all we were designed to be. And we owe it to others to use our gifts to inspire, lift, and support all on their journeys forward.

Today I am empowered to live my life on my own terms. I am at peace with my past. And I am empowering others to see their full potential and aspire to greater or extraordinary, as they reset their lives.

LAURA TOOP

BRIDGING THE GAP

www.thelossconnection.co.uk
Laura.bridgingthegap@gmail.com

CHAPTER 14

"You Have Nothing"

Can you imagine your four-year-old nephew starting this conversation with you? 'Auntie Lollipops (aka Me), now that Uncle Chris is dead, you have nothing".

It was Christmas 2015. I was six months into a most unexpected and, definitely, unwanted journey. I had lost my husband, my health, and my career in quick succession. My life, as I knew it, was in pieces. Everything I had worked hard to achieve, all my dreams for the future, gone in a matter of weeks. My life had spectacularly imploded!

I felt I was living in some kind of parallel universe to the one everyone else was living in. I was exhausted, overwhelmed, and lost, uncertain of what, or how to get back to the 'comfort' of the universe I hadn't chosen to leave. I did, indeed, feel like I had nothing. Along with wading through this parallel universe, my mind felt it was, being battered, in a washing machine spin cycle. Any more pressure, from the world beyond, and I would spin out of control. Echoing in my mind, as if on a continuous loop, were my nephew's words, "You have nothing".

My nephew had kindly offered to "look after me for a hundred days". When you're four, it is a long time, but when you're forty-two, it wasn't going to get me much passed March!

I had to do something, quickly.

I knew, from experience, when life had thrown me other, albeit, much smaller, challenges, I had sought out sunshine. Location was irrelevant, I just had to have sunshine. Only then would I allow myself time to rest, space to breathe, and to, simply just be.

On the island of Aruba, five-thousand miles away, I found that sunshine. Of course, two weeks of uninterrupted sunshine! I wanted hassle-free travel; treating me to an upgrade also allowed for my excess baggage, well almost! A nice conversation with the check-in team and my fee was waived, and me and my excess baggage, were on our way. Strange how a conversation, about excess baggage, could heighten my sense of loneliness, but it did. I had never been one to travel light, all those extra, 'necessary' things I usually stuffed in my husband's half-empty suitcase, was no longer an option.

It hit hard. I was travelling alone. Five thousand miles alone, to be precise.

Stepping off the plane, the sunshine I desperately sought greeted me, as did the thirty-five-degree, sweltering heat! All ready and waiting to take me to the hotel, my taxi driver welcomed me to 'The Happy Island' and wished me a wonderful time. In my heart, I knew I was in the right place, if I wanted sunshine back in my life, even if I was only physically bathing in it, for now.

Each day, I would head to the hotel's private island, taking up my position staring out across the ocean, listening to the lapping of waves and distant voices of others, enjoying their holidays. I would switch continuously between reading, crying, and writing down thoughts. It was rather chaotic, but I needed these thoughts out of my head.

It felt awkward, at first, heading to the island alone. I felt all eyes were on me. I felt people wondering why I was on my own, why was I crying, in these beautiful surroundings. Occasionally people talked and made polite conversation with me, it made for pleasant distraction, to have a mindless chat about everything and anything. I would pretend to be whoever I wanted to be. I would share as little or as much as I wanted to. It was rather liberating, to be honest. The staff were the most attentive, working every day, they noticed I was on my own. We began to talk. I listened to their stories about their lives and their families, and I started to share my story. I was beginning to feel I had something more than nothing. They took the time to ensure I had a suitable table, and even created a cocktail, in honour, of me!

The evenings were the hardest. I sitting, at the bar, along with a book and a notepad. This was the town's 'hot spot', You were meant to sip cocktails and listen to live music until the early hours. It was, certainly, not the place for a book and a notepad!

With time, the regulars became more curious. Drinks were offered and conversations started. "Was I writing a book?" "What was I writing about?" And the one I most dreaded, "Why is such a lovely looking lady sitting here all alone?" It would take me back to my nephew's words, 'You have nothing'. I would answer, politely, "I'm having an adventure" or some other, equally fantastical response, to deflect from what I felt was closer to the truth, 'My life is in pieces'. I have flown five-thousand-miles to figure out what on earth I am going to do next as I have nothing'.

Two weeks flew by, I was only just finding my feet. It was too soon to leave. Throwing all caution to the wind, I cancelled my flight home and extended my stay. Who knew how long for? I just knew I had to put together the pieces of my life, for it to be more than nothing.

I'd brought many books with me. I'd negotiated the waiving of the excess baggage fee. Most of the books were fiction and I couldn't grapple with the content; it felt trite, given the circumstances. There was one, a personal development book, that struck a chord. Ditching the fiction, I sought out the local book shop, with a list of title recommendations from the friends I had made, at the bar. It was a turning point for me. I was seeking understanding, seeking inspiration, seeking motivation. I felt desperate to connect with something, anything, rather than the nothingness I was experiencing. I wanted a life beyond boundaries, full of possibilities, to feel truly alive. After all, I had lived the 'socially-expected' life, where did that get me? My husband was still dead. My career was still over. My health was still gone! I had a choice. To choose what next; something for me, something reflecting the very essence of who I am and what was important to me. 'Brand me', as I like to refer to it now.

'Project Me', and more specifically, 'Bridging the Gap' was born at that moment on Arikok National Park, a unique geological, cultural and historical site, on the east coast of the island. Where, along with thousands of other effigies, left as symbols of hope, I, too, now had added my own. I made a commitment to myself about what I wanted for my life. The sunshine I had lost internally, had now begun to be reignited in me.

Roll forward four years. I have moved ninety miles around the M25, bought a house in a town I didn't know, renovated it into a home, made new friendships. requalified as a transformations coach, and pursued building a business I am passionate about.

Have I made wrong turns? Yes. I started out wanting to be a psychotherapist, but quickly realised I would be fifty before I was able to help anyone! Was my intended career change, back at nothing, again?

Have I found it easy? No. Being served an ASBO, on account of a neighbour hearing music through an open window, he believed to be mine wasn't one of the more joyous moments I had hoped for moving into my new

115

home. Were my newly acquired friendships, back to nothing, again?

Have I wanted to give up? Many times. A year into a much-delayed, renovation project, my builder declares he is bankrupt. I stood staring at a mere shell of a house. Was my home reduced to nothing, again?

Since Aruba, I have learned plenty. However, it was the compassion, respect, and kindness shown by the people there, which gave me the space to begin to understand, to find my voice, and to reconnect with myself and the world again. The woman I reconnected with and how I wanted to show up in the world, having learnt her power for herself, is the very essence of my business 'Bridging the Gap' and how I support others, both professionally and personally.

I would like to leave you with these final thoughts, from the lessons I learned.

If you feel all is lost, and you feel nothing is left. Pause for a moment. You do have something. You have you. You can choose to bring about the change you wish to see. You can choose to live life on your terms, to embrace your natural gifts and passions. Focus your time and energy here, rather than on things simply to 'fit in'. Treat others as you, yourself would wish to be treated, with compassion, kindness, and respect. Offer them space, for their voice to be heard without judgement, expectation, or criticism, in which they can flourish too. You will be richly, rewarded. I have been. People and possibilities will enter into your life, lifting you, beyond anything you could have dreamed of.

Just remember, you, are never nothing!

LISA MARIA COBBLE

EXCEED COACHING LTD

Exceed-coaching.co.uk
lisa@exceed-coaching.co.uk

CHAPTER 15

Every Dog Has Its Day

I have read, listened to and watched many people's stories where they have triumphed over illness (mental or physical), tough situations or harrowing ordeals. They may still be going through it. Many a time I have sat and thought, 'have I got a similar locker of pain/suffering to share?'. I decided that if I had to ask myself, then I mustn't have. More recently, I have cast my thoughts a little deeper and realised that I have brushed with bullying, with sexist remarks or verbal abuse, but what I have surmised is that, whilst I have experienced such things, they were mild and I have never let them get to me.

One situation when I was an engineering apprentice has given me the title to this story. A man who led a department on the shop floor treated me like one of the boys when I was in overalls, then one day, when I was in the office (in a skirt and blouse) he called and asked for me to 'waggle my little ass' to his office with some paperwork. I rose to the bait and went to his office fuming! When he had calmed me down from his 'joke' he said to me, 'every dog has its day'. This has stuck with me forever.

Since then, I have been nominated as best apprentice twice, awarded best overall performance on my master's degree course, continued to get awards, bonuses and deliver on complex projects to go above and beyond. I have not stopped learning or striving for better.

So, to the man that said that.... thank you. It has fuelled my fire ever since.

At the time of writing I have been working on the same site for almost 25 years. I have been through an apprenticeship, via roles in testing, project management, process management and development, business improvement and knowledge management. I have 'volunteered' as the lead of a health initiative and now lead our STEM activities on site. I have thrived on the additional leadership opportunities. My passion shines through. I can be relentless (and almost 'too much!') for some when I get going. I want to succeed and deliver for those I support.

My biggest passion, love and desire is to help people. I want everyone to be happy. I naturally care and support others. When people tell you that you have saved their life, and you don't feel you did anything special, you know you have a calling that cannot be ignored.

Since this 'dawned' on me, I have studied coaching and neurolinguistic programming. I bought my company name on my 41st birthday and I have embarked on developing programmes to coach for careers and retirement. I focus on the client becoming a Superhero, because I believe that everyone deserves the right to feel like a Superhero.

I want to plant seeds for others to grow. I see my coaching style as the planting, and my clients grow from the focus on themselves. Often, they have put their own needs to the back of the pile to look after others. Now, with the attention on them, they bloom to their full potential. They discover a drive and passion that ignites their renewed energy towards a goal. They thrive.

This reflects my own journey. At the start of my career, I was excited to do something different (as a girl) and follow in my Grandad's footsteps, to become a draughtsman. I really enjoyed my apprenticeship (they were some of the best days of my life!). My first job after that was in the mechanical lab where we measured noise and vibration of steam turbines. It was great as there was always something to learn. However, it was not meant to be, restructuring meant I had to find another role. This allowed me to venture into project management in a limited contract position. I loved the change and took charge of working directly with suppliers, sending 40ft containers full of pipes and supports to China. That role started to come to an end so I moved again, applying for a PM role in another business segment. I didn't get that role (as they'd already earmarked someone) so I was offered a different role instead, in Sales support. I then proceeded to teach the person who got the PM role how to use the systems he needed!

Ironic in a way, but it gave me wings to better things. I moved fluidly through roles, adding in additional IT budget management, my master's degree, six sigma green and black belts, and other mini projects. I was becoming someone who enjoyed a lot of variety and spinning many plates. This business segment gave me the space to grow and with the right management, I was given a coach and a mentor, and I really started to fly.

I got projects I could 'run with' without interference. I attended meetings in the boardroom, flew internationally to connect with colleagues and I was in my element. My wings were growing.

I found my way into a secondment to a new part of the business, with some of the previous management team, and used my skills in a Knowledge Management role. During that time, I was asked to support the Customer conference we were to hold in Lisbon, Portugal. It rather quickly turned into me leading the whole event management. I put 110% effort and some into that event. It was magnificent and one of my career highlights. I managed to fall pregnant while in the midst of organising the event (did I mention I like to spin plates?) so, afterwards I went back to the Knowledge Management role until the day I walked out and had my daughter (literally - but that's another story!).

While on maternity leave my previous role was removed and I went back into Project Management when I returned. I had process management / development / improvement, IT tool development and business change management tasks and became the global expert on them all. This was the role I stayed in for 8 years, due to it morphing into bigger things every time the organisation changed. I took on the additional role of coordinating the Project Quality team (more plate spinning) and travelled more with them across Europe.

Throughout my career I have always sought out additional tasks on top of my day job and today is no exception. I am a very active STEM ambassador and I started my own business. I often spin so many plates I should be in the circus. I feel I must add here I am not a jack of all trades and master of none. I am often complimented by others with words such as 'I don't know how you do it all'. Then they read my LinkedIn article about the Power of Productivity, and get an incline as to how the magic works. Between that and high energy ability to focus and learn, these are the secrets to my drive.

My dream is to be so successful in my own business, helping so many people, that I can leave my day job and focus on using my talents freely. For that to happen I will follow my own advice, build the plan and work hard towards it. I am 100% dedicated to making it happen. Now, more than ever, many people need that support.

On this journey, I have also learned the value of saying no. No, is very powerful in protecting yourself against too much, against overwhelm and against being steered away from the true path. I used to say yes to everything then think how I could accomplish this later. It has stood me in good stead providing lots of experiences and learning, and I do still suffer from this 'magpie syndrome' today, except these new shiny opportunities can help support my business and my quest, so they are allowed! Honest! And as we know, I am a master plate spinner.

None of what I do would be possible without another plate spinner in my life. My wonderful husband of 19 years has stood by me, supported me, helped me in ways he will never realise and spins his own plates to keep the foundation of my life solid. I very much appreciate what we have and will protect that above all else.

My advice to anyone who feels they have reached a point in their life when their foundations are set and they have time to branch out or move in a different direction or spin more plates themselves is 'go for it'. You never know where you will end up. There are no regrets from trying, no lessons learned in 'what if's' and no one else to do it for you. Ignite your passion, believe in the power of dreams and live your best life. Make the eulogy of your life a colourful array that all will remember forever and spend a long time recapping at your funeral!

If you need help, you know where I am, ready to spin plates with you.

Every dog will have its day.

MAYA MENDOZA

Psycho-spiritual Therapy | Author | Healer of Stress,
Phobias, Trauma, PTSD, Addiction

PEE STING
MAYA MENDOZA

Peesting.com | maya@peesting.com
Mayamendoza.com | maya@mayamendoza.com

CHAPTER 17

Acorns To Oak Trees

These days children in high risk situations are generally quickly identified. 60 years ago, domestic abuse and mental health were taboo subjects. Indoor violence and bullying, especially in wealthier households, was rapidly and thoroughly hushed up.

A child prodigy, born with an eidetic and echoic memory, my video recorder mind recorded it all. I was a storehouse of classified, behind closed door bumps, bruises and bullying that no one talked about. In bed at night I would sleep with my side light on, one ear open like a cat ready to leap under the bed and hide when the shouting started.

It's been known for years that children who go through high levels of stress and trauma from a young age are wired up a bit differently. Our nervous systems are highly reactive, we are jumpy, easily triggered and riddled with survival and coping mechanisms that can blight us throughout life. Mine started early on.

By age four my unconscious cry for help was obvious. I developed an over eating disorder and got fat, really chubby in fact. As my girth swelled my parents would apologise to people for my size. As they became obsessively fixated with my appearance, the more I felt ashamed and embarrassed. Little by little I shrivelled up and hid inside.

It's a simple truth that "what you focus on grows, what you think about expands, and what you dwell upon determines your destiny". Thus, over three years, under the scrutiny of diet doctors and psychiatrists the problem, me, just got bigger.

With so much attention on the wrongness of my body shape, size, it shouldn't be a surprise to anyone that I grew up into a very angry, insecure and defiant teenager who despised my family and hated myself.

At sixteen I was made homeless. After a few scary nights with nowhere safe to sleep my father found out and put me into one of his bedsits. It was the summer of 1976 and here I was, in a small sparsely decorated room with a single bed, a table, a fitted cupboard and a kitchenette. Somehow, I had acquired two brand new books, Illusions by Richard Bach, and Your Erroneous Zones by Wayne Dyer. As I climbed out of the window onto the flat pitch roof to catch some sun, I had no idea my life was about to change forever.

I think I read those books five times over in as many days. It was like getting an enema for my mind. I was captivated and catapulted into a world where I could knowingly change and master the thoughts in my own head. I could toy with my state of reality and feel into the possibilities that the Law of Attraction could bring. Within this new awareness I felt some form of control - life was guiding me to a route where I could get a sense of a light at the end of the tunnel.

Two years later my father's addictions ended his life. Weeks later my fiancé walked out the door and eight months on I gave birth to a beautiful baby boy. This tiny red headed bundle brought light into my life and sparked a fire in my soul that altered my trajectory. Daniel - Kane as he is known today was the start of everything positive and beautiful that I am and do today.

At this point I had received some grief counselling. Although It helped me unravel a bit, I knew I had just touched the surface. I wanted to be purged of it but I didn't know how to go deeper. In my own search for healing, it slowly dawned on me that I wanted to help others overcome their struggle with addiction. This was the way to release the ghost of my father's malaise within me. The big question was where to start?

A few weeks later I came across a stand at the 1984 Mind Body Spirit Festival in London.

This was my first introduction to NLP (Neuro-linguistic programming). This novel and breakthrough therapeutic technique had just come into the UK. The course on offer was a combination of NLP and Ericksonian Hypnosis. As I sat and watched videos of Erickson and Bandler working with clients I felt an inner spark of hope. This was right for me.

My father had left me a small inheritance and I had just enough money to take the leap and sign up. I took a deep breath, filled in the application form and paid my fee. Thus, began the start of my non-traditional psycho-spiritual education.

Goodness me. What a rollercoaster ride the 12-month training turned out to be. Where I had been stuck and narrow in my thinking and emotions, I became untethered. And here I was, just 22, training with seasoned psychiatrists and psychologists - all of us working together, immersed in a hot house of change.

My fellow students didn't see me as a "problem child". They saw me as they saw themselves, innovators and explorers in mental health. We were breaking through psycho-therapeutic barriers.

Within this intense learning environment, I could become more of my true self. As I began to feel safer my primary coping strategies were exposed and released. My defences dropped and I was able to let people in. I discovered that vulnerability is a gift and a blessing. What a revelation.

My first therapy practice started almost by accident. I had volunteered to work for the British Heart Foundation teaching relaxation and stress management classes to stressed out bankers and financiers in the City of London. The most rewarding aspect of this was seeing the difference a simple 45-minute breathing and visualisation class could do to turn a frown into a smile.

In the next two years I became big fish in a small pond. I had access to a pool of willing clients and forward-thinking therapists that would hang out with me on weekends. Just for fun we would experiment with new therapeutic techniques and ideas and grow and expand in consciousness together. So now I had evolved from a damaged child into a psycho-spiritual innovator playing with a team of exceptional Wisdom Seekers and loving every minute.

During this halcyon period my intuitive abilities exploded exponentially. When it came to helping others my energy simply flowed. I gained a reputation as a shaman and energy healer and my practice expanded effortlessly. I wrote my first book. Started my first Mastermind group. Ran regular healing retreats. Got picked up by Breakfast TV shows and became a mini morning celebrity.

And then disaster struck.

It was predictable really. You see our deeper human psyche is conditioned to hold us within a defined status quo. Whenever we overstep the boundaries of our child-hood identities, self-sabotage kicks in and pulls us back into that defined zone.

Think about it like this: A troubled, problem child can't be a brilliant, ground breaking innovator. A sinner can't be a saint. A survivor can't be permitted to thrive. They are conflicting identities. They don't gel and can't exist in the same space.

From a medical perspective I had an illness that defied diagnosis. My symptoms were so debilitating and all-encompassing that for the best part of a year, and for most days, I was barely able to get out of bed.

So here I was, stuck in the middle of an internal psychological tug-of-war. My body was brought to its knees, and my career ground to a sudden and juddering halt.

In my quest for recovery I discovered that family influence went deeper than I thought. Yes! Genetic Memory is a real thing, and studies show that past generations can (and do) adversely influence our attitudes, health and emotions. Additionally, they impact our capacity for happiness and success. Perhaps this was the scientific expression of Karma? Whatever the explanation, I was done with it.

Fast forward to today. I feel blessed to live a life of mental and emotional grace and ease. My practice attracts my ideal clients without the need for marketing. I have a new business that's starting local and growing global. We positively impact the lives of women, improving their health and wellbeing and saving lives. You can find us at www.Peesting.com. I'm grateful to say my life feels like a privilege and gets better every day.

What I've learned working with thousands of people over 35 years is that to one degree or another we are all afraid of failure. We all have something to hide. We all feel shame and guilt, and have a story where we get to be the victim and blame others for our shortcomings and pain. We all cling on to what's safe and familiar. We all avoid change. We all put on a brave face to hide what we don't want others to see in us. To sum it up, our human experience, whatever our life story, means that emotionally and spiritually we are all the same.

Wherever you start in life has no real bearing on where you finish. Success and failure come in varying degrees and both are inevitable. If you know what you want in life and you are willing to do what it really takes to get there it will be yours.

The key is to recognise we can not transform our lives on our own. We all need help to see our blind spots and remedy those facets of ourselves that act as a barrier to our dreams.

NICOLA HANCOCK

NH BUSINESS GATEWAY

nhbusinessgateway.co.uk
info@businessgateway.co.uk

CHAPTER 18

Crikey - Mum & Dad Look Where I'm Going Now?

The birth of NH Business Gateway began with me wanting to build a better life for myself and achieve inner peace.

At the tender age of 19 I went to work for a global Construction Company. I love engaging with people, in general, and embraced my role as a Receptionist / Support Secretary to the PA. The telephones were rapid, and my organisational skills had to kick in to deliver the caller to the correct contact. This was not just putting a call through unannounced, I had to find out who they were, where they were from and if it was a Director being asked for, then what was the reason for them calling. I had to announce the call clearly and concisely to all contacts within the company. Putting calls straight through just wasn't the etiquette.

Eventually, telephone voice recognition was an additional skill I developed, I was proud of this because it always ensured I sounded friendly and approachable.

I worked for this company from 1989 to 2002, however I had not realised the depth and breadth of my communications skills. I simply took the skill for granted and never appreciated how I delivered and held myself whilst communicating.

In truth I have always struggled within the employment world, mainly due to an invisible condition which sits under the Equality Act and is protected from any discrimination. Being Epileptic (nocturnal partial absences) within the employment world is so misunderstood and different managers have different perspectives on your ability and intelligence. However, I soon came to realise you cannot control how people perceive you as a person and whether they choose to put any 'condition' before you. Basically, I am me "Hello" and not the condition. This was back in the late 80's and all through the 90's, so understanding and being understood with such a broad condition, which is resistant to medication, was a big ask for some very programmed and closed minds.

Unfortunately, discrimination does take place and many times, whilst employed, I found myself coming out of my corner speaking up for myself, pointing out any real unfairness.

The type of things said to me were:

"No, you wouldn't be able to do that"

"You don't have the technical ability to do Customer Service"

"The problem with you Nicola is that you don't accept your own limitations"

"It's not normal"

"You can't travel because of the risk"

The list could go on.

Discrimination for many invisible conditions exists, some choose an indirect way and others are blatant enough to directly discriminate.

Following my time at two large companies, where with both I was made redundant, I applied to work at one of the UK's largest organisations. I commenced in October 2007, I thought of all the places to protect me this would be the one as they proudly showed their Equal Opportunities badge.

My time there was not a positive one, in some area's discrimination was massive compared to previous companies. With my invisible condition I'm dependant on medication, so at times I needed the odd day off. It would appear within the workplace an odd day here and there is more punishable than having multiple chunks of sickness off.

It took me eight years to win my right for 'Reasonable Adjustments' and eventually after some meetings, my flexible working was granted. Unfortunately, this still caused problems and intense observation from any manager.

In my disillusioned mindset, I began to realise how much I was missing my communication skills. This was when I realised how I had taken my skills for granted and how I missed the flow of communication on the telephone and face to face. I felt something was missing and I didn't enjoy being mis-managed by people. I'd always flourished under good leadership, but this seemed few and far between.

I thought about what I really used to love which ultimately took me back to my former construction days, and unbeknown to me a Sales Director, flew across from Dubai on the back of a recommendation to meet with me. It was an evening meeting and I remember him saying "Nicola you can sell, you just need to believe in yourself".

It was only a small opportunity back in 2014 but it was a start and also it was my own little project I could slowly build on, so my fresh adventure had begun on the side whilst I worked 16 hours at this large organisation.

Upon commencing work with him, he purchased a new laptop, 365 Outlook, funded training and before you knew it, I was up and running. Looking back now, what an opportunity and start he gave me.

Once he had taken me on and success was flowing with regular appointments, I was approached by two more global construction companies.

Unfortunately, in 2016 I dropped my UAE client base because I wanted to concentrate on offering my service to the UK. In hindsight I regret dropping these clients, but the cost of ringing the Middle East was no longer cost effective.

I realised I needed a name and a website, so the name NCS Services was formed. It is based on the initials of my maiden name, I didn't realise NCS Services was also a government site, so I think I sat on page 5 of Google.

The website was difficult to convey because I'd never really thought about a website and I was so naive. My NCS Logo was created as part of a skill swap with a marketing agency who created it within 30 minutes. Again, money was an issue so admittedly NCS Services as a name was my first error and a costly one too.

Having dealt with two suppliers who didn't understand what I offered I had learnt a massive lesson, if the expert in the skill your seeking, cannot reiterate back their understanding of what your business is all about – then stay clear and do not use them. Someone who understands will always respond to clarify their perception – listen to what they say, and you will know if they really understand.

I eventually won my first UK client and as time has passed, I've been very fortunate to have worked for larger companies. The amount of times I've wanted to throw in the towel and leave it is beyond belief, but the problem I have is 'this is my baby', I created it from a seed and I've grown it.

In 2016 I rebranded with a designer. It took some time to match what I offered as a Sales and Marketing service to a name. We finally agreed on NH Business Gateway and my logo was created.

I've spent a lot of money perfecting my brand and my personal brand, I'm still not there, but I always remember my Dad saying, "Rome wasn't built in a day Nicola".

By 2018 I finally became totally disillusioned with the company I was working for and decided to take the plunge into full self-employment. I left with a massive amount of fear, but I also had 2 International clients waiting in the wings. My self-talk went "Nicola, you either pack in your business, or you walk away from negativity and use all your positive energies wholeheartedly into growing your business".

I did just that - I wanted the flexibility, the balance and ability to work around the condition. I needed to look after Nicola and I've never regretted it.

My journey has been immense, and I've learnt so much through making mistakes and sometimes being impulsive, spending money I didn't really have.

What I've noticed about my journey into business is how I've grown as a person. I feel I'm far more giving, patient and understanding. Every uphill struggle has been a blessing because as the business woman I have now become I've made it my goal for NH Business Gateway to be mindful, supportive and always wanting equality to be one of its main core visions.

Sometimes I look back and think blimey – look what you have achieved. The sad part is my Mum and Dad are not here to see my achievements after watching my continual struggles with school, medicine and hospital admittances. In fact, they had a few scary moments with me and if they could see where their youngest is now, considering their own battles around the misunderstanding surrounding this and a Headmaster not wanting to teach me within my primary years, I'm sure they would be So Proud!

Finally, my advice to all those managing an invisible disability – be true to yourself, dig deep and strive to put yourself in a place where mentally you can get the best out of life. It may seem hard but please do not worry what others think, the more you worry about ignorance and arrogance the more negative it will be. Be your own genius, discover your talent and skill, as you deserve to be successful and happy without anyone holding you back......Always Shine!!!

PHOENIX MADLEY

Oracle Card Reader
VISIONARY HEART

Visionary-heart.com
visionaryheart@yahoo.com

CHAPTER 19

The Lotus And The Mud

Now we are both here I suspect I better say something. My name Is Magyani Phoenix, some people still call me by my birth name of Laura. Our names are powerful things. They embody who we are. Words can absorb right into the pores of your skin. In some way when you read you take in part of that person. For me, the idea of business, summed up a woman in high heels, and a short skirt. Or someone in a suit. There I was in in my jeans and t-shirt. Spreading my creative blogs, quotes and personal life all over Facebook. It was something I wasn't meant to do you see. Nor share the rawest, most vulnerable parts of myself with the world. Yet I do that. As for me being authentic is my life.

Usually, people took one look at me, saw my arms covered in tattoos and labelled me a trouble maker, Or an unprofessional, person. Many business people, had called me that. I wasn't on their most admired wanted list. Their hit list maybe. Yet, I was now the best voted tarot card reader year of the year in all of Oxford for 2020. As voted by corporate live wire in the Prestige awards. I had two publications in a magazine and over 40 reviews and some were recommendations on the writing of this, on my website

I don't do the whole crystal ball thing. The future is something you create with every choice. I live in a quiet flat with two pet rats. However, that is just currently. And for the last nine years, almost nine years I have attempted to deliver a different kind of Oracle card reading. I believe new models of understanding could be created about business. Ones that go beyond image, competition and the meaning of the word profit.

What we define as a profit in the world. Is purely an individual thing? Why does profit have to be something Financial in nature? So, then I fathomed, what if Visionary heart, the name of my business could make a profit of another kind. For me making profit is knowing that what I do gives me meaning and purpose in life. Therefore, I am making an infinite amount of profit. And also knowing that what I do helps those that do benefit from it in their lives. Yet many people won't and don't consider me a business.

You see visionary heart has mainly been none-profit for many years, but I invite people to give a recommended donation of fifteen pounds, if they want to. Yet they don't have to. All I ask is that they are honest. My life is regularly filled with people telling me that I should have a set price. If I had a pound for every time someone told me that. I would be rich. Yet a person's value isn't estimated by the sum of how much they earn or even charge. Worth is something that you self-design and other people contribute to. That's not to say I won't charge in the future.

I remember the toughest periods of my life without people to turn to. And what I really needed to hear, was: 'You don't have to face this alone'; 'Whatever it is, I can't fix your problems, but here is how I can be here for you'. Yet we all need to hear that at times, don't we? In much of the world, support is given to others if you pay a price. Should this always have to be so? For so many revealing their inner core of feeling, and emotion, their vulnerability, insecurities in a confidential space, which is then free of judgment, can be hard. Yet I believe it could be natural. Where it's natural to embrace emotion and feeling. People then can reveal their most hidden parts of themselves; talk about their aspirations and goal; invite who they want to be, to come out and shine, beyond the mask they think they need to be for others. I offer a space where people can find those things out for themselves. In life, guidance isn't about someone knowing what is best for you. It is about going within and deciding what that is for yourself. Where your meaning arises from the inspiration of yourself. Not what society has chosen for you.

I had gained my wisdom from life experience. It's so true that a part of us is forged in our struggles. And life is defined by your own meaning. Like the lotus, which grows in the mud. We learn from our unfortunate circumstances. We learn to face the world courageously, full of feeling and share who we have come to be, which is always ourselves. We are not here to get rid of the realities of life. Struggle is part and parcel of being alive. As is joy and happiness.

Visionary heart was birthed in my mother's bedroom. The shame, at the ripe age of 31 in the year 2012, having to move back home after being unable to hold down a job, and as a result, losing my privately rented accommodation. I was registered as homeless. I had suffered a massive nervous breakdown.

I had also moved around most of my childhood when my mother remarried someone in the military, when I was 11 years old. I had been to 6 schools, and it was a constant experience of unpacking and packing my life into boxes, moving every few years. I lost count of the many homes I lived in. Many overseas. I moved back to the United Kingdom by myself in 2001, living in house shares.

My self-development started around the age of 22 after a suicide attempt and being diagnosed with clinical depression, which I overcame. I built up my skill base. I had already walked away from high school with exceptional high grades and an award signed by the military for taking care of youths of military parents, and an award signed by the president of the United states, Bill Clinton. I spent time working in everything from factories, to care homes, support work and care work. After the breakdown that occurred many years later, I was a broken person. I used my own self-therapy to help myself.

As I recovered, I used self-therapy to really connect to people. I sat with the homeless, the drug-addicted, ex-criminals, Travellers, the young and even the elderly. I took on bereavement care volunteering and visited others in their homes. I would trade Oracle card readings for a cup of coffee. As the only income I had was from the benefits system, it was a long struggle to rebuild my life, and I did. But if there's one thing I learned, it was that it has to come from you. No one can save you. They can give you tools, listen to you, have understanding. In those times, God was closer than ever to me, because I realised that what I called God was something that existed in myself as the creative force of my own life.

It was through resilience, and self-belief that I built myself back up. I opened up to the greater recesses of my unconscious mind, the voice of Archangel Michael and so much more during the breakdown.

Whatever you deem spirituality to be, I see it as the deeper parts of the mind that know the yearning of your own heart. In turn, I offer people that through my readings, as in a place to find their own voice, because when we deeply listen to others, as much as they are invited to listen to themselves, we learn how to be intimate with ourselves, with God, life and the Universe.

I remember one day looking down, when walking outside. I had been standing on a little sticker with a picture of a Phoenix on it. Who can rebirth themselves in every situation but ourselves? By striving to forge a relationship with change, befriending difficulty when it happens, and transforming it and ourselves, as we have to ultimately live with ourselves. In turn, this becomes how we relate to others. We can face the dark and find our own resources of hidden potential within it. As those things need the light of our awareness. Authenticity, being real is the greatest thing that you can offer the world.

Business is not another place for me to sell something, even if I did charge. Instead It's an expression of the deepest heart of me, where I can encourage others to also remove their masks, rather than just create more. Always head in the direction of life. Self-employment, running a business will mean whatever you want it to mean.

As Archangel Michael would say. 'where you go, life goes. Make things all bright and beautiful'. For they recognise each other as partners. 'For the eyes were given to see, as you were given to life.'

RACHEL HAYWARD

MD | Owner
ASK THE CHAMELEON LTD

Askthechameleon.co.uk
rachel@askthechameleon.co.uk

CHAPTER 20

The Entrepreneurial Magpie

I was 41 when I became self-employed – accidentally, and certainly NOT as part of my game plan.

I am of serial entrepreneur stock, but always determined to be employed – the memories of never having access to the phone for more than 2 minutes at a time and hastily arranged one-week holidays were still strong in my mind! Besides, I was working in the charity HR sector, and pretty much working as an in-house entrepreneur, so the pressure was similar, but the personal risks and responsibilities were fewer.

Bit by bit, I moved from HR into the operations side of my charity employer, writing and delivering contracts, creating a special trading arm, which became increasingly successful.

Soon, we were **flying,** and I had helped create a wonderful team, supporting people who had been out of work. Then austerity hit. One by one, instead of finding people jobs, I was making them redundant, and then it was my turn. When I was 18 at University, I had set my target to become a Managing Director by 35 (without really knowing what that meant) and now I had achieved it. But what next when you've reached your ultimate career goal? My 40th year was not turning out well.

I confess to being very low when I was on my own and generally a bit lost. Like so many, I did a great job of presenting a positive, confident external persona, but looking back, I was struggling.

Fortunately, I'd been lecturing at a University on a casual basis for six months, delivering employability modules to 1st year business students. Could I become a full time academic? No, too soon. Surely, there was another path?

At this critical point in my business journey, a business friend asked me to write a bid for them, which I did, and blow me down if it didn't win! And just like that, self-employment began. With increasing regularity, others made contact. I kept my lecturing contract going and built up my customer base.

I began corporate networking - so very different to that in the charity world; mainly men in grey suits talking about golf (this was 2013!) and, in truth, it was terrifying. I hid behind my phone, trying to look busy, when in fact I looked just plain rude! Eventually I found a welcoming group, hooked up with some inspiring business people, learnt their networking skills and developed a killer pitch. I was growing in confidence and suddenly, I felt I belonged. And I was winning new business!

Eighteen months later, buoyed by my successes, I created Ask the Chameleon, a consultancy of one (me!) poised to take over the world one funding pot at a time.

Why funding?

Well, as an HR professional, particularly in the charity sector, I spent most my time writing policies. In my first charity role I discovered that I had a knack for funding applications, at a time when sourcing grants and funding had never been more important, and very few charities had any expertise in it.

I am also painfully competitive, relishing a challenge, and I **do** like to win. It's my dad's fault; as a young man, he was incredibly sporty (rowing, judo for Britain, rugby, squash) and whilst I am **not** sporty in **any way**, the competitive gene is clearly very prominent in my DNA!

I have always adored words and language. I love a testing word count (nerd), and the freedom that business award applications provide to promote successful people and businesses in ways that they themselves would never feel able to do. We Brits really don't like to blow our own trumpets!

Working alone can be lonely, so I counteract this solitude by surrounding myself with supportive people from business and lecturing. My fellow tribespeople are varied, remarkable, and not just women either – Richard, Bev, Lee, Lindsey, Sharon, Sarah are my go-to-guys. We have each other's backs and are always ready with a helpful suggestion, a positive team chat, or a restorative gin.

You won't win every application, which hurts, especially competitive old me! As a backup revenue stream, I still lecture, remaining part of something completely different and maintaining my HR academic mindset. Time pressures are challenging, but my module leader, Sheena, is SO very thorough and skilled, she makes it easy for me to be involved. I also advise other students on successful networking (ironic, given my early fears!), and my University has embraced this very practical approach to commerce. Networking isn't natural for all of us, and many businesspeople have never had any training. Each year, the students astound me with their new skills – and it makes me proud to see them soar like the network ninjas they have become.

Covid-19 hit my business like a truck. Overnight, 95% of work disappeared. I was left bewildered and heartbroken, and (if I am honest) rudderless. Worse still, I seemed to fall through every single gap available in the Government's raft of support initiatives. I'm not alone in this – an estimated 3m people do too – and the situation is causing irreparable damage for many. I reacted emotionally; I felt this proved that I was not a *real* business, not a *"proper"* business owner, that I was stupid, inadequate and foolish, and I felt ashamed.

It took a good 2 weeks of feeling like this, before I had a good strong word with myself, put my big girl pants on over my trousers and "rescued" myself. No-one was going to save me but me, and I was going to prove I didn't need anyone to do it for me. I reached out to all my eligible business contacts, ensuring they knew about all the sources of support available. I told everyone – family, friends, people I met out dog walking, anyone! Like an evangelistic truffle hound, I was determined to sniff out support for others. I believe this was a turning point in my own recovery. I was determined that this period would not define me.

<breathes, gets off soap box>

This is who I am. Don't tell me I can't, because I can. Don't tell me no, because I'll prove to you (and myself) that the answer can be YES.

The situation has ignited a fire in my belly, giving me a determined, laser focus, which has worked brilliantly so far (still a work in progress, of course).

As always, though, my passion for interacting with people and my magpie-like attraction to shiny new ideas, has kept me looking for pivots and new concepts. And then, I heard a plea for help from a local charity leader for some kind of swapping service.

No time to waste; I joined forces with two local businesses and created Derby Swap Shop. Loosely based on my favourite childhood programme - Multi Coloured Swap Shop with Noel Edmonds - instead of toys and games, we swap skills and services. Maintaining a 70s/80s retro vibe, it was born in the very first weeks of Covid19, and the free-to-use online platform took just 2 weeks to go live!

With over 100 users, 50 regular swaps, and reported business savings in excess of £20k to date, the first 2 months have shown the enormous potential of this novel approach.

It fills me with pride when people tell me they've become a 'swapster', and most often with someone they didn't even know. I might be working like Stretch Gordon, as I juggle my business, lecturing, trusteeship for Annabel's Angels (a small cancer support trust), area lead for the FSB, and now a co-director of Derby Swap Shop Ltd (watch this space for other cities and regions!), but there is nothing more satisfying than poking Covid19 in the eye!

And the future? My ambitions are simple enough;

1. A successful, vibrant Swap Shop in every area, helping small businesses and charities alike.
2. Winning more contracts for my clients – £12m since 2015, and I'm not done yet.
3. To travel and write – I spent 3 months in South East Asia and China in 2009 with my Other Half, James, and I kept a diary. This magpie may be feathering her nest with a fictional book.

And finally, what advice would I give you, knowing what I know now, if I was starting all over again?

You can become a business owner at any time; you don't have to know it all and every conversation you have may lead somewhere, so be kind, friendly and helpful.

It's tough, and you need resilience in bucket loads as you ride the roller coaster. There are things *you* can control, and there will be other things you'll need help with, so **find your tribe**. Search for the right people – kick any doomsayers out of the nest.

And finally, if you're not enjoying it, stop it! Remember, you are your own white knight, rescue yourself and do something else; even if it happens by accident, nothing is forever.

SUE CURR

Mental Wellbeing | Mindset Specialist
FEAR LESS LIVE MORE

suecurr@suecurr.com
suecurr.com

CHAPTER 21

The Wings To Fly &
The Courage To Fall

'**M**orning Sue, sit down, I'm glad you made it.'

It was 9.30am, 26th September 2012 and we'd been here many times over the years. More so in recent months but as I sat down, I could see from the doctor's face that today's visit was going to be different and not in a good way.

Taking my lead from her sombre tone as she cut straight to the chase, I was suddenly aware I was holding my breath.

'There's no easy way to say this Sue but after checking these latest blood tests, I'm going to call for an ambulance"

'Why?"

I didn't need the answer which followed.

I knew why!

But nevertheless, she carried on delivering the verdict that we both knew had been coming for a long time.

'Your latest results show this is serious, your liver is failing, you need to go to hospital, and you need to go now otherwise you'll die and no, before you ask, I'm not joking'.

In that split second the bottom fell out of my world.

I knew that this was it, the carefully crafted façade of the comfort zone I'd been hiding behind all my adult life. The one where I'd been existing inside a mind which had become a prison of my own making during a life-long battle with mental ill-health. The same one which had in the previous fifteen or so years descended into full blown alcoholism and had in one sentence just been spectacularly blown wide apart.

In the split second that she took to deliver the verdict I suddenly realised that I had nowhere to run. Nowhere to hide. I was devastated. Not that I was going to die, that didn't register until much later.

No, it was much more important than that!

It would mean that everyone would know and be able to see me for who and what I was; a mess, a hopeless drunk and they'd hate me for it.

In reality?

Everyone else, already knew me for who and what I was; someone who was extremely ill, struggling to cope, vulnerable and who no matter what, wouldn't let them help me, no matter how hard they tried.

That fact alone was the first of many lessons to come because up to that point in time I was the only one who didn't know that I had a problem – except of course I did!

The rest as they say is history but to cut a long story short the doctor admitted me to hospital and I spent the next six weeks fighting for my life at the end of which and much to everyone's astonishment, I was discharged to the care of my family and sent home to begin rebuilding my life from the ground up.

A life with many more battles ahead in terms of now living with the physical consequences of cirrhosis of the liver and chronic peripheral neuropathy.

But one, nevertheless, which I could now look forward to with renewed optimism, fresh hope, and newfound determination that from that point on, I would live my life in my own way, on my own terms.

In the early days I quickly decided I had to find the courage to be who I really was and quit hiding behind an untold myriad of excuses.

Although I didn't know how, I knew instinctively that I'd pay forward what I'd learned, not only for the greater good of my family and myself but also somehow for the wider world.

I didn't know it then, but I was to become my own 'first client.'

Those next few months were a blur. I was mentally and emotionally drained, but I knew I had a choice to make. I could turn my old fears around to face everything and rise, or wallow in self-pity, continue to fear everything, and run straight back to my old lifestyle.

For the first time in my life I took responsibility for my choices and made a conscious decision to live, truly live, as opposed to continue existing in the shadows of the past. Thus, began the journey to reclaim my life in earnest.

I had no clue at that stage what my new life or the new me would ultimately look like, but I had to start somewhere so I began writing about my experiences. Not a sorry tale of 'why me' more a case of 'try me', as I took the lessons I'd learned during what I've latterly come to call, my 'wilderness years', and used them to best effect in aiding both my physical and mental recovery.

Unlike the 'old me' I embraced those same lessons to finally find the courage to become who I was born to be before life 'taught me' otherwise.

Over a period of about eighteen months people began to take note of what I was saying and I suddenly found myself with an audience, a voice and a platform from which to begin playing forward the message that we all of us can decide to take a chance and choose to change at any point in our lives, in order to effect the long-lasting positive changes, we need and moreover live our best lives possible.

At this point, I hadn't even considered I could take this to the next step and actually start a business. Let alone a thriving business where I could make a positive difference to others just like me by helping them to do what I'd been unable to do for the longest of times.

That being, that they could come to know, own, validate and accept themselves for who and what they are, despite anything, and know that in spite of everything, they are enough!

That was it, I'd discovered within me both a purpose and a passion which in December 2016 saw me take the leap of faith into the world of self-employment.

A decision which I honestly believe has changed my life for the better, forever; One which saw me decide to use my voice for real and move into coaching & speaking.

By nature, I consider myself to be an educator and when I decided to officially move into coaching as a profession, it felt very natural to draw from the professional experience I'd gained whilst working in education and together with the lessons I'd learned on my personal journey, combine the two, to create what ultimately became my hybrid coaching concept Fear Less – Live More.

On September 26th, 2012 I would never, ever have been able to even dream, let alone have the self-belief to make all this come true. Yet today I work with women from all walks of life, coaching them to have the courage to be who they really are. Who they were born to be before the world taught them otherwise, and that my friend makes everything that ever happened to bring me to this point, oh so very worthwhile.

My life today is different in every way to what it used to be. I'm happier, healthier, and more whole than I've ever been but make no mistake about it, just like you I still have days where I want to stop the world and get off because I'm only human after all.

The difference today is that I actively choose not to unpack and stay there because I understand that in everything, absolutely everything, we all of us have a choice.

Going forward, no matter how long it takes for me to actually shake hands with the 'Grim Reaper', I'm going to follow the passion which although borne out of a necessity to survive, has also become my purpose in life. A mission if you will, which sees me spending my life using the voice and skills I now have, to empower others to know, understand and believe that this too can be their truth when they believe in themselves.

If like I once was, you're what I deem to be a 'professional swan' – someone who gives the impression that she's gliding serenely through life without a care in the world, and yet underneath the surface you're paddling like crazy simply to stay afloat for fear of being seen as vulnerable, unable to cope, or God forbid, a 'failure'. Know this my friend, whoever, whatever and wherever you are in this wonderful world of ours, You Are Enough!

You and you alone have the God given right to live your life in a way that sees you happy, healthy, and whole and no one has the right to tell you otherwise.

If you remember nothing else today, remember this, when we believe in ourselves, that self-belief gives us the wings to fly and the courage to fall, safe in the knowledge that we can get straight back up and try again.

Now Go Fly!

EPILOGUE

This book along with Volume One, has given so many a sense of achievement in many different ways.

A journey into your own life can only improve self-awareness and a feeling of triumph on how far you have come. Some have said writing about themselves is a cathartic experience. Others have aligned it with an awakening. Whatever feelings have been evoked; they can only be a step forward in your journey.

Many of these women have become Authors for the first time through their participation in these books. This has also been a stepping stone for some to go on and write their own books.

ABOUT THE BOOK CREATOR

Sharon Brown moved to the West Midlands in 2003 from Glasgow. She worked her way up through various positions and industries and finally started her own events agency in 2015 after a long career in the corporate world. A Qualified Project, Event and Marketing Professional, Sharon seized an opportunity to get online with her business in 2018 after realising a new way of working was needed.

Revival Sanctuary, a global community for women in business was born after some serious soul searching and market research within the women's networking space. Sharon has always understood that in order to get any-where, its far easier and quicker to do this with the right team of people and so the Revival ethos of Collaboration over Competition has been embraced and encouraged throughout the community.

Within this space, new projects have evolved allowing members to work together and to make an income, raise their profiles and increase their brand visibility. One of these projects is MO2VATE Magazine which is a global business bible, aimed at micro and small business own-ers. The beauty of this magazine lies in the article writers who are all business owners so the value is immense to all who subscribe to it.

Another project is The Speakers Index, again allowing members to show their strengths and abilities by working as a team to give opportunities to others who want to amplify their voices within the public speaking forum.

Sharon intends to continue in the online space and to develop more projects like this which can be led by Revival members.

SERVICES

REVIVAL SANCTUARY for women in business is a global community platform operating mainly online. This Exclusive Private Membership Club works efficiently through teamwork and collaborative working practices where projects are created for members to truly embrace the ethos of collaboration over competition.

There are many opportunities including speaking, writing, networking, learning, teaching, and much more.

Contact us at **sharon@revivalsanctuary.co.uk** if you'd like to apply for our membership and visit revivalsanctuary.co.uk for more information on our benefits.

REVIVAL SANCTUARY | FOR WOMEN IN BUSINESS

Revivalsanctuary.co.uk
sharon@revivalsanctuary.co.uk
linkedin.com/company/revival-sanctuary/
facebook.com/revivalsanctuary
Instagram.com/revival_sanctuary
Youtube.com/revivalsanctuary

MO2VATE
THE WINNING FORMULA

MO2VATE MAGAZINE is a business magazine with a global reach. This is written by business owners and is aimed at small business owners. Potential article writers are invited to submit their articles through the website.

Winning article writers are given the chance to appear on the front or back cover, to receive print copies, to be interviewed for our YouTube channel and to become the Editors Choice which will also be showcased on our website. They are also automatically nominated in an appropriate category to our online Awards starting in 2021.

Subscribe at mo2vatemagazine.com

MO2VATE MAGAZINE | THE WINNING FORMULA
Mo2vatemagazine.com
editor@mo2vatemagazine.com
linkedin.com/company/mo2vate-magazine/
facebook.com/groups/mo2vatemagazine
Instagram.com/mo2vate_magazine
Youtube.com/revivalsanctuary

Business Insight
From Olympian to international speaker and TV host! Learn about the mindset needed to make a complete turnaround in your career

One Man's Story
Depression and finding your way back

The fight to survive
How the UK's limited companies have been left behind

Jannette *Barrett*
Celebrates Jamaica's Independence Day and 30 years with her husband Paul by appearing on our cover!

ISSUE 02 | AUGUST 2020

MO2VATE

THE WINNING FORMULA

Social Media: blessing or a curse?
Find out 5 fool proof ways to avoid Social Media distraction

National Bullying Prevention Month:
The stigma around workplace bullying and how you can raise awareness by sharing your story!

Sue
Curr
Our cover girl celebrates 3000 days of sobriety and explains why self care isn't about vanity

ISSUE 03 | OCTOBER 2020

Entrepreneurial Insight:
A look inside the glamorous lifestyle of a Hollywood make-up artist and who was her favourite client!

MO2VATE

THE WINNING FORMULA

SPEAKERS INDEX
AMPLIFYING YOUR VOICE

THE SPEAKERS INDEX is a directory hub to allow speakers to be seen, hired, paid and rebooked.

With social media promotion and a 12-month growth programme on offer, anyone who is looking to earn up to £1500 for their speaking gigs, should join this.

Subscribe at thespeakersindex.com

THE SPEAKERS INDEX | GET SEEN, HIRED, PAID AND REBOOKED
thespeakersindex.com
enquiries@thespeakersindex.com
linkedin.com/company/speakers-index/
facebook.com/speakersindex
Instagram.com/speakers_index

Printed in Great Britain
by Amazon

58096538R00119